How To Books

Finding Voluntary
Work Abroad

Finding Voluntary Work Abroad

All the information you need for getting

valuable work experience overseas

MARK HEMPSHELL
3rd edition

How To Books

Published by How To Books Ltd, 3 Newtec Place,
Magdalen Road, Oxford OX4 1RE, United Kingdom.
Tel: (01865) 793806. Fax: (01865) 248780.
email: info@howtobooks.co.uk
www.howtobooks.co.uk

Third edition 1999

British Library Cataloguing in Publication Data.
A catalogue record for this book is available from
the British Library.

Cartoons by Mike Flanagan
Cover design by Shireen Nathoo Design
Cover image PhotoDisc

Produced for How To Books by Deer Park Productions.
Typeset by Concept Communications (Design & Print) Ltd, Crayford, Kent.
Printed and bound by Cromwell Press, Trowbridge, Wiltshire.

Note: The material contained in this book is set out in good
faith for general guidance and no liability can be accepted
for loss or expense incurred as a result of relying in particular
circumstances on statements made in the book. Laws and
regulations are complex and liable to change, and readers should
check the current position with the relevant authorities before
making personal arrangements.

Contents

List of Illustrations

Preface

There is little doubt that the help of the voluntary sector is in as much if not more demand than ever before. Although the world in general is more prosperous and stable than it has been for centuries there is still no shortage of places around the world where human need is great and growing. It seems that, as soon as one problem is solved, then several more wars or famines break out, and make more demands on the help of the voluntary sector. Even in the wealthiest parts of the world there are still plenty of cases of deprivation, poverty, hunger and disease – and very often found side by side with some of the wealthiest inhabitants of the world.

Many governments around the world have a good record in these areas. Many more do little or nothing to help. In any case, wherever the need arises, the voluntary agencies are invariably there to help. In many ways, the voluntary sector is much better placed to help deal with these problems than any government or official body. UK-based agencies in particular have an excellent reputation for service at home and abroad. It is no exaggeration to say that they are one of the UK's most successful 'industries'!

So, why would anyone leave what is a comparatively prosperous and stable country to offer their services abroad? The reasons are many – excitement, adventure, personal satisfaction, commitment, even religion. None of them are necessarily the only reasons and in their own ways they are all good reasons for volunteering.

One of the main misconceptions about voluntary work that I would like to set aside is that it is totally unpaid, or contributes nothing to an individual's career. Neither of these are necessarily true. Whilst a lot of voluntary positions are unpaid (some even require you to make a contribution to costs) many are paid, if only at nominal rates. And, in fact, there are plenty of positions within the voluntary sector that are paid at commercial rates, including some excellent managerial and executive positions. As something of an industry the voluntary sector needs good people if it is to continue its record of good service.

The purpose of this new edition is to bring you up to date with the latest developments and opportunities in the voluntary sector, particularly changes which have taken place since the last edition was published. The world is changing fast and although the need for voluntary service will probably always exist, the way in which that help is delivered is also changing at speed. In any case, whether you are hoping to make a career of voluntary service, or would just like to spend a few months travelling and volunteering as you go, I am sure it will help you find the opportunity that is right for you.

Mark Hempshell

1
Is Voluntary Work For You?

WHY BE A VOLUNTEER?

Different people give different reasons for wanting to do voluntary work. For some the desire to help others is the main thing. Others do it because a nine-to-five job isn't what they want out of life. For others it is a good way of getting valuable experience that will help them get a job. With the level of unemployment today many people volunteer because a regular job isn't available.

Which of these do you think is the right reason?

The fact is, almost every reason is worth while. You don't even have to have a definite reason. As long as you are genuinely interested in what you do, most voluntary agencies or charities will welcome your application.

WHAT ARE THE PROS AND CONS?

Doing voluntary work always seems like a very good idea. But just because you are working for a good cause does not necessarily mean it is right for you. Many a willing volunteer has caused chaos by volunteering to do the wrong thing.

Voluntary work has both advantages and disadvantages. The main points to consider are these:

The pros

- It can be very rewarding helping others.

- You will learn new and useful skills.

- Experience in voluntary work may impress future employers; it will look good on your curriculum vitae.

- There is often a chance to work abroad, perhaps in countries you would not otherwise have a chance to visit.

● You will get a chance to do things you could never do in a regular job (such as saving lives in Africa or working in China).

The cons

● Some of the work is either unpaid or low paid.

● Some types of work are quite competitive to get into. You might not always get your first choice.

● Some voluntary work involves more mundane office work, administration and fund raising than 'hands-on' work helping others.

● You may have to give a minimum commitment (such as one or two years).

● You may get personally or emotionally involved. It is not 9-5 work.

Only you can decide how much the individual pros and cons matter to you. For example, some people feel that working for a voluntary agency will always be second best to a 'proper' job. For others it is much more rewarding, regardless of what they are paid, and the experience may even help them to get a much better job in future. Take some time to decide for yourself.

WHAT CAN YOU CHOOSE TO DO?

One of the advantages of voluntary work is that there is something for everyone. But you must take care to match up what is available with what you want. One project might be enjoyable for one person, but a nightmare for another.

As one volunteer said, 'It is best if you have a passion for the work you are doing. And don't do it if you don't at least have a keen interest!'

The range of types of voluntary work is very wide. Helping out with a jumble sale or flag day are just two ways, but there are many others too . . . teaching, nursing, building, labouring, office work, fund raising and even just befriending are all types of voluntary work.

There are no divisions to voluntary work as such. But most agencies which have opportunities for voluntary work tend to specialise in a particular type. These are some of them:

Working with the elderly.
Working with children and young people.
Working in hospitals.
Working to relieve poverty.
Working with the disabled.
Working in education and training.
Working in conservation and the environment.
Working with animals.
Working in archaeology and history.
Working with reform and pressure groups.
Working with religious charities.
Working in medicine and health.
Working in disaster relief.
Working to give advice.
Working for peace and development.
Working for minorities.
Working with the homeless.
Working on community projects.
Working with prisoners.
Working with public service charities.

. . . . But really there are organisations doing almost everything!

WHERE WILL YOU DO IT?

There are two choices:

In the UK
You can do voluntary work in the UK, either in your own area or further afield. However, what is available will depend on your area. Some voluntary agencies work nationwide; others only regionally or locally. Most of the larger agencies have their head office in London.

Internationally
Volunteers can work in almost any country of the world. A lot of work is done in the poorer, third world countries by agencies that are based in the richer countries. In general terms there are fewer opportunities to work internationally than in the UK and most of these jobs are for those with experience of voluntary work in the UK.

As another volunteer said, even though you may want to go to a particular country it is more important to choose the right type of work for you than the destination — 'Choose the type of work first, then the country second!'

WHAT SKILLS DO YOU NEED?

Voluntary agencies look for both formal skills and personal skills. The most important formal skills needed, in some but not all jobs, are:

- medical skills
- nursing skills
- technical skills, such as engineering or mechanical skills
- teaching skills, academic and others
- practical skills, such as a knowledge of building
- business skills.

Personal skills are just as useful in voluntary work. For example, if you have a friendly personality, like helping people, and are good at organising things these will all be useful.

It is a good idea to make a list of your own skills, both formal and personal, and then see how you can make best use of them. The skills needed for the various types of work are given later.

WHAT EXPERIENCE DO YOU NEED?

Some voluntary jobs require you to have previous experience in a similar type of work; others do not. Some work experience in a commercial business or industry is almost always useful in voluntary work. Also, if you are looking for a paid voluntary job then experience in an unpaid voluntary job will help.

It is a good idea to make a list of any work experience you have, or think what experience you could get. This is particularly important if you want to do voluntary work straight after leaving school or college. See the Planning Chart at the end of this chapter.

WHAT QUALIFICATIONS DO YOU NEED?

There are no special qualifications or courses in voluntary work available in the UK at present. Most employers look for individual skills and experience instead and you can apply for most jobs without any qualifications at all. But remember:

- Some jobs require a good general education. This usually means four or five GCSEs, including English and Maths.

- Some jobs require a degree from a university.

- Some jobs require a vocational qualification. For example, a qualification in social work.

If you are choosing subjects at school or college, check now that you are taking subjects which will help you. Some information on particular qualifications is given here and you will find more information later on.

Medical qualifications

If you want to work as a doctor you must hold a degree in medicine. Courses are offered at a range of universities in the UK; details are available at careers libraries.

There are also opportunities for people with other medical qualifications to work for voluntary agencies. These include chiropody, dietetics, occupational therapy, physiotherapy and radiography. Further information is available from:

The Society of Chiropodists, 53 Welbeck Street, London W1M 7HE.

The British Dietetic Association, 22 Suffolk Street, Queensway, Birmingham B1 2LS.

The College of Occupational Therapists, 6 Marshalsea Road, London SE1 1HL.

The Chartered Society of Physiotherapists, 14 Bedford Row, London WC1R 4ED.

The College of Radiography, 14 Upper Wimpole Street, London W1M 8BN.

Nursing qualifications

If you want to work as a nurse you must be qualified, holding either a nursing degree and/or state enrolment. There are opportunities for those with qualifications in general, sick children's, mental and mental deficiency nursing.

Details of courses are available at careers libraries.

Some jobs involving work with children ask for a nursing/childcare qualification such as the NNEB (Nursery Nurses Examination Board) diploma. Details are available from CACHE, 8 Chequer Street, St Albans, Hertfordshire AL1 3XZ.

Social work qualifications

If you want to work as a social worker you must usually hold a CQSW (Certificate of Qualification in Social Work), CSS (Certificate in Social Service), SQASW (Single Qualifying Award in Social Work) or the Diploma in Social Work. Degree courses in Social Studies are also offered by some universities and colleges.

Information about training as a social worker can be obtained from the Central Council for Education and Training in Social Work, Derbyshire House, St Chad's Street, London WC1H 8AD.

Teaching qualifications
If you want to work as a teacher you must hold a qualification. Various types are available and details are available in the *Handbook of Degree and Advanced Courses*. In Scotland, details are available from the Teacher Education Admissions Clearing House (TEACH), PO Box 165, Holyrood Road, Edinburgh EH8 8AT.

Conservation work
A range of qualifications is available if you want to work in conservation. These are provided by universities and colleges and include Countryside Management, Environmental Studies, Ecology, Zoology, Biology or Natural Sciences. Details of all the available courses are contained in the *Directory of Environmental Courses* available from The Environmental Council, 80 York Way, London N1 9AG.

Veterinary work
If you want to work as a veterinary surgeon you must study at veterinary school and be registered with the Royal College of Veterinary Surgeons. Further details are available in a booklet called *A Career as a Veterinary Surgeon*, available from the Royal College of Veterinary Surgeons, 32 Belgrave Square, London SW1X 8QP.

Degree courses in the subject are offered by universities at Bristol, Cambridge, Edinburgh, Glasgow, Liverpool and the Royal Veterinary College, London.

Veterinary nursing
If you want to work as a veterinary nurse you should follow an approved training course. Details of courses are available in a booklet called *Veterinary Nursing*, available from the British Veterinary Nursing Association, Unit D12, Seed Bed Centre, Coldharbour Road, Harlow, Essex CM19 5AF.

Archaeology and history
If you want to take a job with an agency involved in archaeological or historic work, you may wish to study for a degree in Archaeology, Archaeological Studies, Archaeological Science or Ancient History. More information is available from the Council for British Archaeology, Bowes Morrell House, Walmgate, York YO1 2WA.

Legal work
If you want to undertake legal work with a voluntary agency, you must usually hold a degree in law. These are offered by most universities in the UK.

Further details of all courses and qualifications can also be found in careers libraries.

WHAT ABOUT LANGUAGES?

It is always useful to have some knowledge of a foreign language for voluntary work, especially if you want to work abroad. If you have some knowledge of a language, say so when applying for a job. That said, it is not always essential to know a foreign language, even for some jobs abroad. English is very widely used in the world of voluntary work.

Remember: the more you have to offer, the better the choice of work you will have, particularly when working abroad.

Ask yourself this question: What have I got to offer a voluntary agency?

SOME OTHER THINGS YOU SHOULD KNOW

Can anybody get voluntary work?

No. Most voluntary agencies receive many applications and can afford to pick and choose their volunteers. There is a lot of competition for paid jobs in particular and many applicants are unsuccessful. Also, whilst the agencies always appreciate genuine offers of help, they can easily spot and reject those who are looking for a free ride.

How long will I work for?

Most longer-term jobs require a minimum commitment. This might be a number of weeks or months or a minimum number of hours per week. Most full-time jobs are for a minimum of one year, and two- or three-year jobs are common. Sometimes the paid jobs only last for as long as the agency has funds to pay your wages.

Do I get paid?

Most voluntary agencies will employ both paid and unpaid workers. Which you choose will depend on your own personal requirements and situation but, either way, this is something you should check at the outset.

Paid work

In this case the pay will be similar to that you would receive working in a similar job for a commercial company. For example:

— Full-time office or shop manager £15–£18,000 per year.
— Full-time fund raiser £12–£18,000 per year.
— Administrator £10–£18,000 per year.

— Social worker or support worker £15–£25,000, depending on experience.

Unpaid work

If your job is unpaid you might still get travelling expenses and 'pocket money', up to around £25 per week. If the work is residential, where you have to live in, accommodation and food are usually provided free.

These rates are for jobs in the UK. In a foreign country you will be paid local rates. These may seem small (such as £2–£3 per week), but in countries with low living costs (such as Africa) may actually be quite good.

Will I have to contribute anything?

Yes, it can cost you money! In some cases volunteers in unpaid jobs are expected to make a contribution to do voluntary work. This can range from £25 for a weekend conservation project to £500 for a summer-long project in Europe.

If there is no charge as such you may still have to pay your own travel and insurance costs, or even accommodation costs.

Will I need any permits or visas?

Visas or work permits are not needed by citizens of one European Union (EU) country doing voluntary work in any other EU country. The EU countries are Austria, Belgium, Denmark, Finland, France, Germany, Greece, Italy, Ireland, Luxembourg, the Netherlands, Portugal, Spain, Sweden, as well as the UK.

If you want to do voluntary work elsewhere you will normally need a visa and work permit. Obtain details from the appropriate foreign Embassy. Their addresses are given in Chapters 4 and 5. Usually visas and permits for voluntary jobs are granted much more easily than those for other jobs.

What about tax and national insurance?

Voluntary workers must pay tax and national insurance contributions on their income just as with any other job. This applies even if you are working for a charity. Also, even if you are working abroad you are liable to UK taxes if you are still officially resident in the UK.

If you are working in, but not actually a permanent resident of, a foreign country, you will not usually be able to use any local health and hospital facilities free of charge. So, it is important to arrange your own health and travel insurance before leaving. Some voluntary agencies provide this free for their employees, but others do not.

What about voluntary work for the unemployed?

Unemployed people can do voluntary work for voluntary organisations and still claim Jobseeker's Allowance. However, they must still be available to look for and take up a paid job at short notice, which means that they cannot take long-term voluntary jobs. If you are paid more than a very small amount you will lose some or all benefit.

There are different arrangements if you want to work on a short full-time project at home or abroad. Up to 14 days can be taken once each year without it affecting your claim even although you are not actually available for other work during that period. Ask your Benefits Agency Office for details.

What happens afterwards?

A proportion of voluntary jobs come to an end eventually, such as when a particular project has finished or funding for that post runs out. (Most voluntary agencies would be more than happy to disband should there no longer be a need for their services.) Not all volunteers go on to another project. Some go back to work for commercial businesses. This is known as resettlement.

Most voluntary agencies devote much effort to helping their employees resettle. Some pay a resettlement grant or bonus. Many provide counselling and advice for some time after you have finished a project. Two organisations which assist and bring together ex-volunteer workers are:

Returned Volunteer Action, 1 Amwell Street, London EC1R 1UL. Tel: (020) 7278 0804.

Christians Abroad, 1 Stockwell Green, London SW9 9HP. Tel: (020) 7737 7811.

Generally, voluntary work gives good experience for work back in business and industry and will benefit your CV. But not all employers see it this way. It is a good idea to think about what work you will do afterwards and choose voluntary work that will help towards that as much as possible.

PLANNING CHART

Types of work preferred:

1st _____

2nd _____

3rd _____

Destinations preferred:

1st _____

2nd _____

3rd _____

Skills required for your preferred types of work:

_____

Do you have these skills? If not, how can you obtain them?

_____

Experience required for your preferred types of work:

_____

Do you have this experience? If not, how can you obtain it?

_____

Qualifications required for your preferred types of work:

_____

Do you have these qualifications? If not, how can you obtain them?

_____

Languages required for your preferred types of work:

_____

Do you speak these languages? If not how can you learn them?

_____

2
The Main Types of Voluntary Work

It's not enough just to have a vague desire to do voluntary work: you will have to be quite specific about the type of work that most appeals to you.

This chapter breaks down the range of work available into three broad groups:

● 'hands-on' work that helps people directly

● work that helps people by trying to change their circumstances

● work that improves the environment and our understanding of it.

These are followed by a brief description of the types of job offered.

'HANDS-ON' WORK WITH PEOPLE

Working with the elderly

What you do
Most countries of the world have an increasing elderly population. In many of them government-provided services, where they exist at all, are failing to keep up with the needs of elderly people. This situation is expected to become even more severe in the future. Voluntary agencies have stepped into the gap in many places and they provide financial help, various practical helping-hand services and even just companionship.

Work with the elderly crosses many different fields. For example, it can involve medical and nursing work, work with the disabled, or work with the poor elderly. Some jobs with elderly people may even involve no work as such, other than just being a companion and a friend to talk to.

Jobs	*Could you do it?*
● Social worker	_____
● Case worker	_____
● Companion/carer	_____
● Support worker	_____
● Advice worker	_____
● Unit manager	_____
● Unit worker	_____
● Specialist workers: doctor, nurse	_____

What you need

A nursing qualification is required for nursing jobs. A social work qualification is required for social workers. However, the main requirement for work with the elderly is a degree of patience and understanding of the concerns and problems that older people face. Many younger voluntary workers find this hard. Some prior experience is very useful in getting a job, such as part-time work in a nursing home.

How to find a job

These types of jobs are most usually advertised in local newspapers. If not, make a direct approach to employers.

Jobs in this type of work fall into three categories:

● The first is work in nursing homes and sheltered accommodation operated by private companies.

● The second is with local authorities which provide residential homes, day centres, home carers and social workers. Your local telephone directory is the best source of addresses; also try the *Municipal Yearbook and Public Services Directory*, available at main reference libraries.

● The third type of work is with voluntary agencies in the UK and abroad. These are listed later in this book.

Pay and conditions

These vary greatly according to the type of job. A companion/carer may be paid £3.60 per hour; a qualified social worker up to £20,000 per year. The main thing to note is that these jobs require a regular commitment, as an elderly person may come to rely on you. You cannot just give it up.

Where to find out more

Local authorities are a good source of information. The main charities can also supply details of their work. Help the Aged raises funds for work with the elderly in the UK and abroad, partly through its network of charity shops. Age Concern works on practical projects such as day centres and home visiting. Other large agencies which work with the elderly include the Anchor Housing Trust, the Sue Ryder Foundation and the Salvation Army.

Working with children and young people

What you do

Voluntary work with children and young people is some of the most demanding but rewarding voluntary work. It is suitable for both young voluntary workers and older people who may be able to share their experience of looking after their own children.

This type of work is very wide ranging and once in one sector most voluntary workers tend to specialise, although it is possible to change. The main areas of work are special needs teaching; social work; health services; group leading and sports/activities instruction; residential home care.

Jobs   *Could you do it?*

- Social worker   _____
- Case worker   _____
- Teacher/tutor/instructor/youth leader   _____
- Unit manager   _____
- Unit worker   _____
- Specialist workers: nurse   _____

What you need

Many of the jobs in this type of work need formal qualifications. Social workers and teachers must usually have a degree as well as a social work/teaching qualification. Unit managers should also have a social work qualification. Youth leaders must usually have a properly recognised sporting qualification.

At the very least you must have some experience. Not everyone can get on easily with children, particularly those with special needs. Many nursery schools, primary schools and special schools welcome part-time helpers.

How to find a job

Look in the local press and national press, or approach employers direct.

There are three main sources of work. The first is with local authorities which run various residential homes and special schools. The *Municipal Yearbook*, available at all main libraries, lists these. The children's charities also recruit. Some of these are listed later in this book.

As well as charities, some voluntary service bureaux can offer work with children. More information about these bureaux, and contact addresses, are given in Chapters 3 and 4.

Pay and conditions

Most full-time jobs require qualifications and commitment and so pay more than many other jobs. A unit manager earns from £20,000 per year.

Those working with children are usually carefully vetted and must not have a criminal record. In many jobs of this type smoking and drinking are not permitted during duty hours. Many jobs in residential homes are live-in, or require sleeping-in two or three nights each week.

Where to find out more

Contact charities direct. Local authorities and special schools may also be able to help. The main charities in this area are Barnardo's and National Children's Home which offer residential care. The NSPCC provides a social work service. Save the Children Fund operates projects in the UK and 30 foreign countries. ChildLine provides an advice line and counselling service. TocH provides activity programmes. The Salvation Army also works with children.

Case history

Susie Ford: information officer, children's charity

'As an information officer I'm not directly involved with the children. I provide an information and enquiry service at our head office. If a member of the public writes asking for information about us, or a journalist needs information for an article, then I'm the one they speak to.

'My previous job was as a secretary, so I was completely new to the world of charities. But I don't think you would get a job like this unless you found out what the charity did and believed in their aims. Before I applied I got all the booklets and brochures I could from the local library and carefully read up on what we do.

'This is a jobshare post; a lot of charities let you do this. I and my colleague, Anna, work 20 hours a week each to make up one full-time job. There's some flexibility to adjust the hours and days to suit ourselves.'

Working in hospitals

What you do
Hospitals use a large number of voluntary staff. These are quite separate
from the medical and service staff and generally provide extras for
patients which wouldn't usually be available. You might provide drinks to
visitors or a library trolley service, raise funds, or just be a bedside visitor. Hospital radio station work is also available.

Jobs   *Could you do it?*

- Social worker   _____
- Companion/carer   _____
- Project organiser   _____
- Fund raiser   _____
- Support worker   _____
- Specialist staff: hospital radio DJ or engineer   _____

What you need
Experience or qualifications are not needed for most voluntary work in
hospitals. A knowledge of hospitals or experience in business is useful. A
cheerful personality is a must.

How to find a job
Such jobs are rarely advertised. You should write or telephone all your
local hospitals. Contact the administrator, the voluntary services organiser or league of friends.

Pay and conditions
Most of these jobs are unpaid. Some jobs such as social worker or project
worker may be paid.

Where to find out more
Contact the National Association of Leagues of Hospital Friends and The
National Association of Hospital Broadcasting Associations.

Working to relieve poverty

What you do
Even in the wealthier countries of the world, there are many voluntary
agencies whose aim is to relieve poverty. This is done in a variety of ways.
Some give practical help or money to the poor. Others provide self-help
and education. Others concentrate on raising funds. A large number of

agencies do not provide direct help but instead concentrate on promoting the issues and lobbying governments for more aid or changes in the law.

Jobs	*Could you do it?*
● Social worker	_____
● Case worker	_____
● Project leader	_____
● Project worker	_____
● Information officer	_____
● Administration officer	_____
● Project organiser	_____
● Fund raiser	_____
● PR/Publicity officer	_____
● Researcher	_____
● Lobbyist	_____
● Advice worker	_____
● Campaign staff	_____
● Programme manager	_____
● Specialist workers: lawyer, accountant	_____

What you need
Most jobs require no specific qualifications or experience, although experience in business is often useful and some senior staff require a degree. People who want to work in this field should have an understanding of the issues surrounding poverty including unemployment, low pay, welfare benefits and the poverty trap.

How to find a job
Jobs of this type are usually advertised in the national newspapers; also apply to voluntary agencies direct. Some local authorities also offer employment opportunities in this field.

Pay and conditions
A project manager on an overseas aid project would typically earn £25,000 per year and be employed on a two- or three-year contract. A researcher with a UK charity would earn approximately £14,000 per year.

Where to find out more
Contact voluntary agencies direct. The main agencies, working in the UK and abroad, are CAFOD, Christian Aid, Oxfam, War on Want, World

Vision and the Salvation Army. The Child Poverty Action Group and Low
Pay Unit are agencies which provide information and undertake research
and publicity on poverty.

Working with the disabled

What you do
The voluntary agencies which work with the disabled are some of the
most progressive. Most of them work on the basis of self-help and
voluntary workers are employed to support disabled people rather than
do everything for them. The work more often involves teaching, guidance and social work rather than, for example, cooking or cleaning.
People in this field work in residential homes, day centres and clients'
own homes. Many disabled people actually participate in voluntary work
themselves.

Jobs	*Could you do it?*
● Social worker	_____
● Case worker	_____
● Companion/carer	_____
● Teacher/tutor	_____
● Administration officer	_____
● Fund raiser	_____
● Support worker	_____
● Advice worker	_____
● Unit manager	_____
● Unit worker	_____
● Specialist workers: doctor, nurse	_____

What you need
Some jobs require specialist qualifications. Medical staff must be professionally qualified. Teachers usually require special needs training. Social
workers and unit managers require social work qualifications. Other than
this all applicants must have an understanding of the needs and problems
of disabled people, and the wide range of disabilities. Some residential
homes and day centres welcome part-time helpers, which could provide
valuable experience.

How to find a job
Jobs in this field are advertised in the local and national press and the
Community Care and *Disability Now* journals. As well as voluntary
agencies local authorities and hospitals also recruit for this work.

Pay and conditions

A support worker in a residential home earns up to £16,000 on average. A unit worker could earn in the region of £14,000 per year, although many unpaid volunteers are recruited for this work. Most positions demand a regular commitment in that a disabled person may come to rely on your support and companionship.

Where to find out more

Contact the voluntary agencies. Some of these are Barnardo's, the Leonard Cheshire Foundation, RNID, RNIB, PHAB, SCOPE, Guide Dogs for the Blind, MIND and MENCAP. Other voluntary agencies, such as Age Concern, Oxfam and the British Legion, also work partly with the disabled. RADAR is an organisation which co-ordinates the work of over 500 organisations.

Case history

John Greaves: support worker, London

'I work for a charity which runs several homes for the mentally handicapped. They're not great, rambling institutions, but small places that are as much like a real home as possible.

'Support worker is the right name — because I'm here to support our clients, not look after them. Support work is all about finding out what they want to do and helping them to achieve it. So, for example, if a client wants to go shopping it would be the easiest thing in the world to go out and do it for them. We don't do that. Instead we make sure that they know what to do and where to go and then leave them to it as much as possible. So they can be as independent as possible.

'Of course, it's a very rewarding job and we get a lot of affection from our clients. They see us more as friends really. This isn't a residential position, but I'm required to sleep in once or twice a week, which all goes to make it more of a vocation than just a job.'

Working with the homeless

What you do

Homelessness is a growing problem in the UK and many other countries worldwide. Various organisations operate in this area, mostly in hands-on work, including providing food, clothing, temporary and permanent accommodation and advice on rights and benefits. Some also offer education and resettlement. A small number of jobs are available in administration and fund raising.

Jobs   *Could you do it?*

- Case worker   _____
- Project leader   _____
- Project worker   _____
- Project organiser   _____
- Support worker   _____
- Advice worker   _____
- Unit manager   _____

What you need
Specialist skills and qualifications are often useful but not usually essential. Experience in business or a knowledge of law, rights and welfare benefits, housing legislation, or a social work qualification, is needed in some jobs. An understanding of the causes of homelessness and a genuine willingness to help are the most important things.

How to find a job
Jobs are advertised in national and local newspapers. Also approach voluntary organisations direct. If you want to work abroad, contact agencies and the voluntary service bureaux. Jobs are available both with charities and with local authorities.

Pay and conditions
A significant number of workers in this area are unpaid volunteers. A homeless persons officer with a local authority, or the manager of a hostel, could expect to earn £14–£18,000 depending on experience. A few jobs are residential or semi-residential.

Where to find out more
Organisations involved in this type of work include Homes for Homeless People, National Children's Home, Shelter, Simon Community and the Salvation Army. There are also local organisations in most areas. Obtain details at your local library. In London some of the main organisations are Alone in London Service, Centrepoint Soho, SHAC and Piccadilly Advice Centre.

Working in medicine and health

What you do
Medical charities are a small but important part of the voluntary work scene. They work at different levels and in various different types of

work. For example, St John Ambulance is mainly a local organisation, whilst the Red Cross works right around the world.

You may help to provide medical care and health services. However, many agencies are involved with disaster relief or providing other support services wherever a need or problem exists. Some agencies do no hands-on work but are concerned with fund raising or promotion.

Jobs	*Could you do it?*
● Social worker	_____
● Case worker	_____
● Companion/carer	_____
● Project leader	_____
● Project worker	_____
● Support worker	_____
● Unit manager	_____
● Specialist workers: doctor, nurse, other medical specialists such as radiographers, physiotherapists, laboratory technicians	_____

What you need
Many of these jobs will require specialist qualifications, such as in medicine or nursing. In the others some experience is preferable. This might include work in a hospital, clinic, local government or business. Unqualified people mostly work in administration and fund raising roles.

How to find a job
Contact the voluntary agencies direct. Some jobs are advertised in the national newspapers and employment agencies sometimes have vacancies. For work overseas contact voluntary service bureaux. Foreign governments also sometimes know of vacancies in their countries. Contact them through their London Embassies.

Pay and conditions
Pay for most jobs ranks equally with the commercial sector. Contracts of employment are usually for a fixed period of one or two years. Some agencies have opportunities for qualified people to undertake sabbaticals of several weeks or months, or work during their annual leave.

Where to find out more
The main charities include the Red Cross, Médecins Sans Frontières,

Save the Children, the Salvation Army, Oxfam and ATD Fourth World. Work is also available through Voluntary Service Overseas (VSO) and the government-sponsored Overseas Development Administration (ODA), and United Nations organisations such as UNICEF and UNHCR.

Working with religious charities

What you do
It is important to note that there are two types of work done by religious organisations. Some of the work is religiously motivated, similar to missionary work. However, this is much less usual today. Agencies run by religious organisations usually perform some hands-on work which supports the principles of their faith. Often this involves working with the poor, elderly, young or homeless.

Jobs	*Could you do it?*
● Case worker	_____
● Project leader	_____
● Project worker	_____
● Project organiser	_____
● Fund raiser	_____
● Support worker	_____
● Inspector	_____
● Programme manager	_____
● Unit manager	_____
● Researcher	_____

What you need
The main point about working with religious charities is that you must usually follow that religion yourself and have a proven track record – perhaps of attendance at the relevant church, where appropriate. Those who are selected for paid jobs almost always have some previous experience of unpaid voluntary work. Other than this there are no specific requirements, although specialist skills can always be used.

How to find a job
In the first case ask the relevant church or group for information or advice. They will usually know what jobs are available, or where to contact, and they may be willing to give you a referral or reference. Alternatively some jobs are advertised in the national press.

If you want to work abroad contact the relevant organisation or the voluntary service bureaux. Again, it will help to have a reference from the corresponding organisation in the UK.

Pay and conditions
Although some jobs with religious organisations offer commercial rates of pay, many others are partly paid or unpaid. However, they usually offer full accommodation, expenses and pocket money, especially if working abroad. Most jobs are for a fixed contract length ranging between 2–3 months and one, two or three years.

Where to find out more
Contact your church or religious organisation direct. Some of the main agencies are the Salvation Army, CAFOD, Pax Christi, Christian Aid, TocH, Methodist Homes for the Aged, the Church Army and Jewish Care.

Working with disaster relief organisations

What you do
The work of disaster relief agencies is always important, although many agencies whose brief is to provide emergency aid for disasters find their help is needed on a permanent basis. Oxfam, for example, was initially formed to respond to one disaster but now maintains a permanent presence in several locations.

Some of the work offered by these agencies is hands-on, such as delivering food aid or providing medical facilities. In these cases planning, management and organisational skills are needed much more than practical labour. Most of these agencies also have a very large fund raising and promotions operation.

Jobs   *Could you do it?*

● Project leader   _____
● Project worker   _____
● Information officer   _____
● Administration officer   _____
● Project organiser   _____
● Fund raiser   _____
● PR/Publicity officer   _____
● Support worker   _____
● Programme manager   _____
● Specialist workers: doctor, nurse   _____

What you need

Most jobs with disaster relief organisations require a high degree of competence. Most personnel are educated to degree level. Experience in a business environment is preferred and experience in transport, agriculture, education, health and infrastructure is useful. Knowledge of one or more languages (such as French, Spanish, Arabic or an African or Asian language) is often needed.

How to find a job

Contact the voluntary agencies directly. Some vacancies are advertised in *The Guardian* and *The Times*. Foreign governments also sometimes have these vacancies. They can be contacted through their London Embassies.

Pay and conditions

Many of these jobs pay comparable rates to executives in commercial business. A programme manager in Africa may earn £25–£30,000 per year or more. Most of these jobs are on fixed term contracts of one, two or three years. If working abroad the work may have to be undertaken in difficult or dangerous conditions.

Where to find out more

Agencies involved in this type of work include the Red Cross, Care, Christian Aid, Help the Aged, International Rescue Corps, World Vision, the Ockendon Venture and the Salvation Army. The government-sponsored Overseas Development Administration (ODA) also works in this field.

Case history

Andrew Wright: programme manager, Africa

'As programme manager my job is to manage the whole programme that our charity operates in this area, which expands over three countries. It's very wide-reaching. Initially we came here to relieve famine conditions and to get in enough food, clothing, medical supplies etc to keep people alive. But we're not just a prop. We'd like as much as anyone else not to be here. So we're involved with such things as building wells, trying to get crops established, building homes and training local people to set up medical services. In other words, self-help.

'This job is on a two-year contract. It wasn't possible to bring my family, but I do receive paid-for return trips home each year. We're working in pretty difficult and dangerous conditions. My job involves a lot of office and management type work, but it's definitely not an office job!

'So, how did I get here? I originally worked in industry in planning and development. Then I came out to Africa with VSO for one year, just to take a break and add to my skills. At the end of the project I saw this job advertised, applied, and got it. If this contract isn't extended I'll aim to get another job with a charity because I've decided this type of work is definitely for me. However, I can always go back into industry and I think it is always useful in this type of work to have that option. But will there ever be a day when charities aren't needed?'

Working in prison visiting

What you do
A small but important aspect of voluntary work is prison visiting. Several organisations provide the visitors, volunteers to organise activities, social workers and teachers. There are also several voluntary agencies which help ex-prisoners with advice and practical help regarding their accommodation, employment, training and welfare benefits.

Jobs	*Could you do it?*
● Social worker	_____
● Case worker	_____
● Teacher/tutor/instructor	_____
● Project leader	_____
● Project organiser	_____
● Support worker	_____
● Advice worker	_____
● Unit manager	_____

What you need
Most jobs require no specific qualifications except that teachers and social workers should be appropriately qualified. Other than this an understanding of the problems of prisoners and ex-prisoners and a genuine willingness to help are most important.

How to find a job
Contact the voluntary organisations direct. The national organisations may be able to put you in touch with local groups. Some jobs are also advertised in the national and local newspapers.

People who want to become prison visitors should contact the governors of their local prisons.

Pay and conditions
Many jobs in this area are for unpaid volunteer visitors. Rates for paid
staff are similar to other voluntary agencies. Many jobs require a regular
commitment and work in the evenings and weekends.

Where to find out more
Agencies involved with this type of work include the Apex Trust,
National Association for the Care and Rehabilitation of Offenders
(NACRO), National Association of Prison Visitors, National Association
of Probation Officers, Prisoners Advice and Information Network,
Prisoners Wives and Families Association, and Catholic Social Service
for Prisoners.

WORKING TO IMPROVE PEOPLE'S CIRCUMSTANCES
Working with reform and pressure groups

What you do
Reform and pressure groups are a particular type of voluntary agency.
They do not usually carry out any hands-on charity work. Instead they are
concerned with promoting a particular cause or getting a particular
message over. This may be aimed at the public, or it also may be aimed at
governments and other influential people. For example, Amnesty
International campaigns for human rights. The Campaign for Freedom of
Information is working towards a public right of access to official
information.

Jobs   *Could you do it?*

- Information officer   _____
- Administration officer   _____
- Project organiser   _____
- PR/Publicity officer   _____
- Advertising & marketing   _____
- Lobbyist   _____
- Campaign staff   _____
- Programme staff   _____
- Researcher   _____
- Specialist workers: lawyer, accountant   _____

What you need
Experience in business or some type of office work is desirable. Many
people have previously worked in the advertising industry or the media.

A degree in a relevant subject, such as business studies, marketing, media studies or social science is sometimes required. You must usually agree with the way in which the issue is being promoted.

How to find a job

These jobs are advertised in the national newspapers, frequently *The Guardian* media section or *Campaign* magazine. They may also be handled by employment agencies.

Pay and conditions

These are similar to rates of pay in the advertising and newspaper industries. A PR officer might earn £15–£25,000 per year, depending on experience. A researcher (with a degree) could expect £16–£20,000.

Where to find out more

Contact the reform and pressure groups and also other voluntary agencies which have a PR or marketing department. Agencies include the Electoral Reform Society, the Howard League for Penal Reform, the Campaign for Press and Broadcasting Freedom, CND (Campaign for Nuclear Disarmament) and the Runnymede Trust (campaigning against racism).

Working with advice and counselling organisations

What you do

There are plenty of voluntary agencies who do no actual hands-on work as such but specialise in giving advice to the public at large or particular groups. Some of these, such as the Citizens Advice Bureaux, have come to be regarded as a public service although they are still largely voluntary agencies.

The main types of work with these agencies are social work and office work; this involves receiving and processing enquiries from clients and trying to offer a satisfactory solution. These agencies also undertake research and collection of information, publishing, fund raising and campaigning. Some operate advice hotlines, counselling services, and friendship groups.

Jobs	*Could you do it?*
● Social worker	_____
● Case worker	_____
● Information officer	_____
● Administration officer	_____

- Fund raiser   _____
- PR/Publicity officer   _____
- Advertising & marketing   _____
- Lobbyist   _____
- Advice worker   _____
- Unit manager   _____
- Researcher   _____
- Specialist workers: lawyer   _____

What you need
Very few of these jobs require formal qualifications. Experience in business or the civil service is useful. Those applying for paid jobs will benefit from some prior experience in unpaid voluntary work. In the UK, knowledge of an Asian or African language is sometimes needed. Having said this, most organisations will train people to provide the service they offer. Applicants must be able to get on well with different types of people.

How to find a job
Jobs are advertised both in the local and national newspapers. Otherwise, contact the voluntary agencies direct. For work abroad, contact the voluntary service bureaux in the relevant country.

Sources of this type of work include both charities and most local authorities.

Pay and conditions
Voluntary agencies in this sector use many unpaid voluntary staff. Those who are paid often receive slightly less than for similar jobs in industry. For example, a unit manager might earn £15,000 per year. An advice worker might earn £11,000 per year. Often these posts are for a fixed period of one or two years and cease when funding for them runs out.

Where to find out more
Organisations undertaking this type of work include Help the Aged, MIND, Runnymede Trust, ChildLine, Relate, Students Nightline and the Samaritans. The National Association of Citizens Advice Bureaux acts as a central body for local Citizens Advice Bureaux. Some local authorities, colleges and universities, and commercial companies also provide these services. The Advice Services Alliance (ASA) works to represent individual services.

Case history
Janey Stewart: welfare advice worker, Glasgow
'My task sounds simple but can get very complicated. I visit people who've called into the advice bureau and help them make sure they are receiving all the benefits to which they're entitled – and the right benefits. It's not a job the Department of Social Security can do themselves, which is why people turn to charities like ours.

'I've got to keep on top of the rules and regulations of all the welfare benefits and any changes in the law. I've got a good working relationship with the DSS – that's where I worked before I took up this job. Other than being a walking encyclopedia of benefits I don't have any formal training or special qualifications.

'My work involves seeing people in the office and travelling out all over Glasgow. Many of the people I see are trying to get by on a tiny amount of money each week and it's very rewarding when I can get them extra benefits which they are fully entitled to but which they just didn't know how to claim! In other cases it can be very frustrating because not every case is cut and dried and we get claims and negotiations with the DSS stretching out for weeks – then I get blamed for it.

'At the moment the bureau has funding for my post for another two years. Because there's so much to do it will almost certainly be extended beyond that, but there is a certain amount of insecurity with this type of job.'

Working for peace and development

What you do
A number of organisations are working for peace on a worldwide basis, and for the advancement of less developed countries. Although these agencies do provide some hands-on help in the third world countries, much of their work is office based and involves organising community projects, lobbying governments and bringing the issues to the attention of the public.

For example, Third World First (3W1) exists to develop awareness of poverty and injustice worldwide. International Voluntary Service (IVS) organises workcamps worldwide in which people can come together to understand each others' cultures and work on a practical project.

Jobs   *Could you do it?*

● Project leader   _____
● Project worker   _____

- Information officer   _____
- Administration officer   _____
- Project officer   _____
- PR/Publicity officer   _____
- Lobbyist   _____
- Campaign staff   _____
- Programme manager   _____

What you need
A committed interest in peace and development is essential in this type of work. Many full-time staff have a degree in social studies or a language, although this is not essential. Experience in business is useful for some of the jobs.

How to find a job
If you want to work in the UK or abroad with UK agencies then apply direct to the relevant organisations. Very few jobs are advertised as such. If you want to work abroad apply direct to agencies in those countries or voluntary service bureaux. Some addresses are given in Chapters 4 and 5.

Pay and conditions
These agencies use a high proportion of unpaid voluntary staff. Paid staff can expect similar rates of pay to those in other agencies. Most jobs are for a fixed period of six months to one year, especially if working abroad.

Where to find out more
Some agencies involved in this type of work are Amnesty International, Peace Advertising Campaign, Peace Brigades International, Peace Pledge Union, ATD Fourth World, Co-Operation for Development, Third World First, International Voluntary Service, Women's International League for Peace and Freedom, Campaign for Nuclear Disarmament and War on Want.

Working for minorities

What you do
Work with minorities is an expanding area of voluntary work. There are organisations who work for most people in a minority or disadvantaged situation, particularly on grounds of race, colour, sex, sexual orientation, poverty or age.

The work includes practical hands-on help, particularly teaching,

social work and advice work. However, many other people work in
administration, PR, lobbying, campaigning, research and information.

Jobs	*Could you do it?*

- Social worker   _____
- Teacher/tutor/instructor   _____
- Information officer   _____
- Administration officer   _____
- Project organiser   _____
- PR/Publicity officer   _____
- Lobbyist   _____
- Support worker   _____
- Advice worker   _____
- Campaign staff   _____
- Researcher   _____
- Specialist workers: lawyer   _____

What you need
Some jobs need specialist qualifications but these are rarely essential.
Prior experience in business or unpaid voluntary work is an advantage.
The most important thing to note is that it is often necessary to be a member of the particular minority group in order to be considered. This is permitted by the sex discrimination and race relations laws in many countries
including the UK. If not, you must at least be in sympathy with the problems of that particular minority. Some jobs require knowledge of a foreign
language.

How to find a job
Many jobs of this type are advertised in the national newspapers,
particularly *The Guardian*. Alternatively approach voluntary agencies
direct. In addition, some local authorities recruit staff to work with
minorities.

Pay and conditions
An advice worker would earn in the region of £15–£18,000 per year. A
researcher, with a degree, would earn in the region of £12–£15,000 to
start.

Where to find out more
Agencies involved in this work are mostly small, local organisations.
Information can be obtained from organisations such as the Local
Authorities Race Relations Information Exchange; Liberty, Minority

Rights Group, the Runnymede Trust (race relations), the Institute of Community Relations, and the UK Association of Rights and Humanity.

Working in education and training

What you do
There are many opportunities in education which are not directly connected with teaching in a school. Numerous voluntary organisations work in re-education or training. This might involve helping those with special educational needs or providing training, perhaps as a way of escaping unemployment. Some of the jobs are in organisation or administration rather than hands-on teaching.

Jobs   *Could you do it?*

- Social worker   _____
- Case worker   _____
- Teacher/tutor/instructor   _____
- Project leader   _____
- Project worker   _____
- Information officer   _____
- Administration officer   _____
- Unit manager   _____
- Unit worker   _____
- Specialist workers: special needs teacher   _____

What you need
A teaching qualification or social work qualification is needed for many jobs in this area. Experience of working as a volunteer in a school or special school would be useful. Experience in business is useful for some of the administrative jobs.

How to find a job
Look in national newspapers, particularly *The Times* and *The Guardian* education pages. Some employment agencies, voluntary service bureaux and Job Centres have these types of jobs. Also contact the voluntary agencies direct.

Jobs of this type are available from three sources. Some are to be had with local education authorities or special schools. Others are with the voluntary agencies themselves.

Pay and conditions
A qualified special needs teacher earns between £15,000 and £28,000 per year depending on specific qualifications and experience.

Where to find out more
Contact local authorities and voluntary agencies. Some educational/train-
ing agencies, and other agencies whose work includes education/training
are Community Service Volunteers and Fullemploy, whose work includes
the training of unemployed people, Royal British Legion, Guide Dogs for
the Blind, Brook Advisory Centres, St John Ambulance and Oxfam. Also,
the University of the Third Age promotes training opportunities for retired
people.

Working with public service charities

What you do
Various voluntary agencies offer what are often regarded as essential public services, when in fact they are entirely run and funded with little or no
government help. Examples here are the RNLI (Royal National Lifeboat
Institution) and the RSPCA (Royal Society for the Prevention of Cruelty
to Animals). These agencies are often run along the lines of large businesses and have large requirements for staff.

Jobs   *Could you do it?*

- Social worker   _____
- Case worker   _____
- Companion/carer   _____
- Teacher/tutor/instructor   _____
- Project leader   _____
- Project worker   _____
- Information officer   _____
- Administration officer   _____
- Project organiser   _____
- Fund raiser   _____
- PR/publicity officer   _____
- Advertising & marketing   _____
- Lobbyist
- Support worker   _____
- Advice worker   _____
- Inspector   _____
- Campaign staff   _____
- Programme manager   _____
- Unit manager   _____
- Researcher   _____
- Specialist workers: including doctors, nurses,
  engineers, scientists, technicians, builders   _____

What you need
Requirements vary considerably depending on the agency involved.
Contact the agency you are interested in working with for details. In most
cases a good general education, experience of working with the public,
previous work experience, and previous experience of unpaid voluntary
work are always an advantage. Most of these organisations train staff to
their own particular requirements.

How to find a job
Use national and local newspapers. Write direct to voluntary agencies. If
you want to work abroad contact voluntary service bureaux and foreign
embassies – addresses are given later.

Pay and conditions
Vary considerably. Some jobs are paid, but others are unpaid or pay
expenses only.

Where to find out more
Agencies involved in providing public services include Alcoholics
Anonymous, Bankruptcy Association, British Pregnancy Advisory
Service, ChildLine, Cruse - Bereavement Care, National Association of
Citizens Advice Bureaux, Law Centres Federation, Relate, Royal British
Legion, the Red Cross, the Samaritans and Women's Royal Voluntary
Service (WRVS).

WORKING WITH THE WORLD AROUND US

Working in conservation and the environment

What you do
Conservation issues have become popular recently and so the number of
opportunities in this work is increasing. Organisations involved in this
divide into two types. Some are involved with promoting and campaigning on conservation issues; others undertake hands-on conservation projects, such as protecting wildlife habitats or restoring canals or footpaths.
A number of agencies do both types of work.

Jobs   *Could you do it?*

- Project leader   _____
- Project worker   _____
- Information officer   _____
- Administration officer   _____

- Project organiser   _____
- PR/Publicity officer   _____
- Lobbyist   _____
- Campaign staff   _____
- Programme manager   _____
- Unit manager (or warden)   _____
- Specialist workers: builder, engineer,
  surveyor, scientist, biologist   _____

What you need

Certain jobs in conservation require specialist qualifications. Scientists, biologists and engineers should usually have a degree in these subjects. Experience in business is useful for those trying for administrative jobs. College courses in Countryside Management, Environmental Studies and Ecology are also available.

All applicants must have a keen interest in conservation issues. Some prior experience on a conservation project is a good idea for those hoping to make a career here. The British Trust for Conservation Volunteers (BTCV) offers 3–12 month periods working as a volunteer officer on conservation projects.

How to find a job

Jobs of this type are mostly advertised in *The Guardian*, environmental section, the BTCV *The Conserver* newspaper, and *New Scientist* magazine (scientific jobs). Work abroad can be obtained through voluntary service bureaux in those countries.

Pay and conditions

A large number of jobs in conservation are unpaid and some short projects require some contribution from the volunteer. A paid project leader or warden would earn around £12–£14,000 per year.

Where to find out more

Useful background information can be found in *The Conserver* newspaper and the BBC *Wildlife* and *Green Magazine*. Some of the agencies involved in conservation include BTCV, the Council for the Protection of Rural England, the Countryside Commission, Friends of the Earth, Greenpeace, the Royal Society for the Protection of Birds (RSPB) and the World Wide Fund for Nature (WWF).

Case history

Graham Jones: wildlife warden, nature reserve

'Originally I trained as a mechanic, and started joining conservation projects as an unpaid volunteer warden, learning about wildlife and conservation as I went along. When the job here came up I applied and got it!

'As the warden I do get involved with some hard, hands-on practical work, such as fencing, tree maintenance and clearing ditches. But a fair bit of my work is managerial and administrative. I have to draw up work rosters for our volunteer wardens and supervise their work, and I'm also in charge of the visitor and school study centre we have. Handling our budget and paying the bills also takes time.

'It's a very unique way of life, but probably not something you would want to do unless you were interested in conservation. My advice to anybody thinking of making a career in conservation would be to sign up as a volunteer on a weekend or week-long project and just jump in!'

Working in national heritage

What you do
Although governments take national heritage more seriously than in the past, this job is most usually taken on by the voluntary agencies. Some of them are involved in hands-on preservation work, on archaeological digs or historic buildings. This work involves excavating, preserving and cataloguing. Other agencies are involved with running historic sites as visitor attractions, such as Stonehenge, and this work involves maintenance, cleaning, security, general administration and management rather than archaeology.

Jobs	*Could you do it?*
● Project leader	_____
● Project worker	_____
● Information officer	_____
● Administration officer	_____
● Project organiser	_____
● Advertising & marketing	_____
● Unit manager (warden or curator)	_____
● Specialist workers: scientist, archaeologist, historian	_____

What you need
Work as a specialist or curator usually requires a degree in a subject such as History, Archaeology, Art, Art History or Museum Studies. Qualifications in subjects such as surveying or construction may also be

useful. Other jobs do not need any specific qualifications, but an interest in history would be useful, and many staff study for vocational qualifications, such as those offered by the Museums Training Institute, once they have found a job.

How to find a job
Jobs are advertised in the local and national newspapers. Alternatively, contact agencies direct. Jobs of this type are available with the voluntary agencies and local authorities.

If you want to work abroad, contact the voluntary agencies and voluntary service bureaux in the relevant country. These are listed later.

Pay and conditions
Many jobs in this sector are for unpaid volunteers and consist of workcamps lasting for several weeks or months. A full-time curator or archaeologist might earn £20–£25,000 per year, although it depends on their individual qualifications and experience and the importance of the site or property they supervise.

Where to find out more
Contact agencies direct, such as English Heritage and the National Trust. The National Trust owns 300 historic buildings and many historic sites. The Museums Training Institute may also be able to help. Most areas have a local historic society (see your telephone directory). *Whitakers Almanack* contains a list of historic monuments, properties and sites throughout the UK. This is available at main libraries.

Working on community projects

What you do
Community projects cover a wide variety of different activities. However, many organisations are working to improve the local community, in the UK and internationally. Projects might include building an adventure playground, running a summer play project on a housing estate, or creating a city farm.

Although there are opportunities for hands-on work here, such jobs are mainly unpaid. People are recruited on a paid basis to plan, organise, supervise and recruit for such projects. This requires skills in planning, organisation, finance, budgeting, purchasing, personnel, and teaching.

Jobs   *Could you do it?*

- Teacher/tutor/instructor   _____
- Project leader   _____
- Project worker   _____
- Information officer   _____
- Project organiser   _____
- Programme manager   _____
- Specialist workers: lawyer, accountant,
  engineer, builder   _____

What you need
Specialist qualifications are required for all the specialist workers. However, they are unnecessary for the other jobs. In this case some experience in business will be useful. Applicants must be able to work with people from many different backgrounds.

How to find a job
As most community projects operate on a local basis look in your local area first. Ask the voluntary agencies and your local authority for advice. Also check in local newspapers for news of forthcoming projects. If you want to work abroad, contact foreign embassies or voluntary service bureaux.

Pay and conditions
A project organiser might earn £18–£20,000 per year. Some jobs may only operate for a period of weeks or months. In this case payment would be on a proportionate basis.

Where to find out more
Organisations involved in community projects include British Trust for Conservation Volunteers, Christians Abroad, Community Service Volunteers, TocH, REACH (for professional people), International Voluntary Service, Skillshare Africa and Voluntary Service Overseas. The National Association of Volunteer Bureaux may be able to advise. Also check with local contacts including local authorities and libraries.

Case history
Vicky White: volunteer co-ordinator
'There's something of a barrier between paid workers and unpaid volunteers in every voluntary agency. My job is to break down that barrier, so we get the best out of everyone that works for us.

'Finding and recruiting our volunteers is quite a lengthy process. First we take out advertising and do public relations (PR) work to get people interested in volunteering. Then we send them our volunteer's information pack with an application form to complete. When a volunteer applies they have to be interviewed and then vetted.

'Once a volunteer comes on board it's also my job to find where we can best make use of them, and where they'll be happiest. Volunteers with business or office experience tend to end up helping with our fund raising. Those with good person-to-person skills are often trained to become case workers or advice workers. It doesn't always work out well and if there's a clash of personalities it's up to me to sort it all out.

'My previous experience was in personnel work with a High Street bank, and actually there's not as much difference between the two places as you might think. We're a charity but we're still very results orientated and have to be very efficient. Anyone who says voluntary work isn't a proper job obviously hasn't done it!'

Working with animals

What you do
Work with animals is one of the most popular types of voluntary work. As a result it can be quite hard to get into. The number of jobs which actually involve working with animals is smaller than the number of jobs available in administration and fund raising. Those jobs which involve working directly with animals are those of vet, veterinary nurse, kennel assistant, or inspector, working in clinics, animal homes and in the community.

Jobs	*Could you do it?*
● Project leader	_____
● Project worker	_____
● Information officer	_____
● Administration officer	_____
● Project organiser	_____
● Fund raiser	_____
● PR/Publicity officer	_____
● Advertising & marketing	_____
● Inspector	_____
● Campaign staff	_____
● Unit manager	_____
● Specialist workers: vet, nurse, kennel assistant	_____

What you need
Some jobs will require formal qualifications and training. Vets must

follow a five-year course at veterinary school. Training courses for veterinary nurses, kennel assistants and animal inspectors are provided by employers such as the RSPCA and local vets, although competition for these jobs is tough. Previous experience of looking after or working with animals is an advantage. Business experience is useful for administration/fund raising people.

How to find a job
These jobs are rarely advertised. If interested you should contact the voluntary organisations and local vets directly to see if they have vacancies.

Pay and conditions
Starting pay for a veterinary nurse is in the region of £5–£7,000, increasing with experience. An animal inspector or home manager would usually be paid in the region of £12–£18,000 per year. Many jobs of this type require you to work for a probationary period of 6–12 months before your appointment is made full and final.

Where to find out more
The RSPCA produces a short booklet called *Careers with Animals*. Some voluntary agencies are the Blue Cross, Greenpeace, National Canine Defence League, the PDSA, RSPCA, SSPCA, RSPB and the World Wide Fund for Nature (WWF).

Case history
Geoff Burrows: inspector, RSPCA
'I'm one of the 300-odd strong team of inspectors employed by the Society in Britain. Our brief is very wide. We investigate any matters relating to cruelty to animals, or just problems that arise with pets or working animals, and then use the resources of the Society to try and sort them out.

'Some of the cases are routine, others quite horrific. One day we might be dealing with a horse that's been left in a field for months without any proper care, or helping the police to deal with a dangerous dog. We also monitor the movement of farm animals in road transporters – sometimes right across Europe – and investigate complaints from members of the public about other people's pets. Although we wear a uniform we're not a police force but, if necessary, we do collect evidence so that offenders can be taken to court.

'The Society has a training course which operates as and when new inspectors are needed. New inspectors must be 22–40 on joining, fit, and with a driving licence. To start with there's a 12-week course at the head office, followed by three months' work alongside a qualified inspector, six weeks back at head office and then a final written exam. New inspectors are on probation for their first 12 months.

'It's not a job you'd do if you didn't like animals. That said, although experience of working with animals is useful, it's experience of working with the public that is the most useful skill you could have here.'

Other voluntary organisations

It is difficult to classify all the voluntary agencies which operate under a limited number of headings. Some agencies do several types of work, and there are always agencies which do not fall easily into any slot. In addition, new agencies are always being formed and existing ones sometimes change what they do.

As a result this chapter should be considered as a guide only. Even if you are interested in one particular type of voluntary work do be ready to consider the others. Indeed consider approaching any voluntary agency to see if there may be a job for you. Details of how to locate any voluntary agency, together with addresses for many of them worldwide, are given in Chapters 3, 4 and 5.

JOB DESCRIPTIONS

What the main jobs involve

Social worker

Social workers must usually be professionally qualified (see Chapter 1). A social worker deals with a variety of social difficulties or needs, including poverty, lack of housing, financial difficulties, drug abuse, child abuse and many others. However, their brief is to look at the overall situation, understand problems and try to solve or ease them in order to improve the overall social situation of their clients.

Case worker

A case worker may be a qualified social worker, but not all agencies require this. A case worker is usually allocated to deal with one specific problem: for example, a need for rehousing or help with finding special educational facilities.

Both social workers and case workers must be able to develop a one-to-one relationship with people they help, who are usually known as their clients, and give close personal support and guidance.

Companion/carer

Needs no special qualifications or experience. Must be outgoing and able to become a good friend to those in need. A companion/carer may help with dressing, bathing, feeding or cleaning, but no special medical skills are usually needed.

Teacher/tutor/instructor
This job category can cover many different types of work including academic, special needs and sports. Jobs of this type always require applicants to hold a suitable teaching qualification.

Project leader
A project leader is allocated to the day-to-day running of a particular product. In practice he or she is a supervisor, supervising the work of project workers and reporting to a project organiser or manager. The job needs good personal skills and good experience of successfully completing any type of project.

Project worker
Works on projects under the supervision of a project leader. Usually no experience or special skills are needed but skills such as DIY skills and a driving licence etc are often useful.

Information officer
Collects, stores and publishes information and makes it available to members of the public, press and other voluntary agency staff. Some information officers have training or experience in journalism, but others come from a general office/administration background.

Administration officer
Does a variety of administrative work. In smaller agencies one person may handle all the typing, filing, book-keeping, telephone and reception work. Experience in business is useful, as is the ability to use a computer.

Project organiser
Is the manager for a specific project. He or she will then arrange the finance, paid and unpaid volunteers, resources such as transport and accommodation and, where needed, publicity for a project. Experience of organising and administration is useful.

Fund raiser
Most agencies employ staff whose only job is to raise funds. This includes organising collections and flag days, advertising for donations, lobbying governments and local authorities for funds, attracting sponsorship and, in some cases, selling products.

PR/publicity officer

Gets information about the agency over to the public by means of publicity/news stories placed in the media. Many PR officers have previously worked as journalists and when they come to work for a voluntary agency have already developed good contacts with the media.

Advertising and marketing

A&M people work on 'selling' the charity. This may include advertising to attract donations or to make potential clients aware of the services that are available. Many A&M people have previously worked for an advertising agency or in the media.

Lobbyist

The job of a lobbyist is to supply information to influential people, such as MPs, MEPs, government ministers, civil servants, councillors, local government personnel and business leaders – and thereby to campaign for changes in law or policy, or alternatively funding. Lobbyists often have prior experience in advertising/marketing, in PR, or as journalists.

Researcher

A researcher investigates particular situations or events and compiles a report on them. This information is then used by other people within the agency for their own work. For example, a PR officer might ask his or her researcher to prepare a report on child poverty in a particular town so that they can then write an article on this for the press. Some agencies train their own researchers and no experience is needed, although experience in the media, or in library work, is often helpful.

Support worker

The job of a support worker is to support the clients of a voluntary agency, such as elderly or disabled people. The work is that of a guide/monitor, helping the clients to achieve what they want to do as independently as possible. The work is not the same as either a carer or a social worker.

Advice worker

An advice worker must be well informed on a particular issue, such as welfare benefits or housing legislation, and be able to give out advice accurately and clearly. Some advice workers have previously worked with a local authority or government department or have a legal background.

Inspector
Inspectors are required by some voluntary agencies to investigate given situations and decide how the agency can help, or how they should react. No specific experience is needed but inspectors should usually be good at dealing with people.

Campaign staff
Campaign staff lead a particular campaign. This might be to raise funds, to publicise the work of an agency, or publicise a particular situation, such as a famine or miscarriage of justice.

Programme manager
A programme manager is something of a department manager and is employed by an agency to oversee a particular part of their activities. For example, to work in a particular foreign country or develop an area of their work, such as work with children or the elderly. Business skills, such as finance, budgeting, personnel, purchasing and marketing, are often useful. Many programme managers are recruited from other voluntary work positions.

Unit manager
Manages a unit, such as a residential home, shop, day centre, wildlife reserve or activities centre. The work requires a range of skills, particularly budgeting, housekeeping and personnel, and often involves more administration than hands-on voluntary work.

Unit worker
A unit worker works in a unit, such as a home, shop or centre, under the direction of a unit manager. A wide variety of different jobs are involved. Some unit workers provide nursing and personal care and may need nursing qualifications. Others are involved in retail work, housekeeping, or administration. In these cases the work is similar to that in a shop, hotel or office.

Agency director
A charity director is in overall charge of a voluntary agency, very much like the managing director of a company. Most charities have a committee or board made up of several directors. Most agencies recruit their directors from experienced voluntary workers, although some recruit directors who have previously worked in or run businesses.

Specialist workers
All agencies have a need for certain specialist workers. These include

doctors, nurses, lawyers, accountants, engineers, scientists and builders. These specialist workers do much the same work for a voluntary agency as for any other employer.

The most important point to note here is that voluntary agencies do not train these specialist workers. People who want to take up specialist jobs with voluntary agencies must first obtain training and experience with a commercial employer and then, once qualified and experienced, apply for a job with a voluntary agency.

3
How and Where to Find a Job

USING UK NEWSPAPERS TO FIND JOBS

National newspapers
A number of vacancies in voluntary work are advertised in the main national daily newspapers.

Each newspaper does not carry a large number of vacancies but, when all the newspapers are looked at together, there is a reasonable number each week. It is unlikely to be worth buying all the newspapers every week; most main libraries have them in their reading room.

Look in the following newspapers for vacancies:

- *The Daily Telegraph* (particularly Mondays)
- *Sunday Telegraph*
- *Daily Mail*
- *Daily Express*
- *The Mail on Sunday*
- *Sunday Express*
- *The Independent* (particularly Thursdays)
- *The Guardian* (particularly Wednesdays and Fridays)
- *The Times*
- *The Independent on Sunday*
- *The Sunday Times*

Local and regional newspapers
Also look at your regional and local newspapers, although the number of vacancies will depend on whether there are many voluntary agencies with vacancies in your area. London's *Evening Standard* usually carries some vacancies of this type and Monday is the main day for them.

Specialist publications
There are a number of specialist trade and other trade publications which

can be used to locate job vacancies both in the UK and abroad. Many of the vacancies they carry are for experienced people, but it may still be useful to read these publications.

Trade publications can be purchased on subscription or read free of charge in the periodicals department of your local large town or city library.

These publications are particularly useful:

● *Community Care*
● *The Conserver*
● *Campaign*
● Church magazines and newspapers
● *Overseas Jobs Express*

Overseas Jobs Express newspaper (out fortnightly) carries some job vacancies in voluntary work, including both casual and seasonal jobs and full-time vacancies. It is available on subscription from: Overseas Jobs Express, Premier House, Shoreham Airport, Sussex BN43 5FF. Tel: (01273) 440220.

NCVO News, published by NCVO Publications, contains news and information for those working for voluntary agencies. Ten issues annually. Details are available from: NCVO Publications, Regent's Wharf, 8 All Saints Street, London N1 9RL. Tel: (020) 7713 6161.

USING FOREIGN NEWSPAPERS TO FIND JOBS

If you want to try and find a job abroad then it is a good idea to use foreign newspapers. As in the UK most foreign newspapers carry job advertisements. You would need to speak the language of that country in order to understand the ads, although some countries, such as Spain and Greece, do have a few English language newspapers.

It is not always necessary to travel abroad to buy foreign newspapers. They may be available from these sources in the UK:

● Newsagents in major cities: however, the cover prices are high.

● Libraries in major cities: some libraries have a limited selection of foreign newspapers.

● Foreign Embassies and Consulates: the UK Embassies of some foreign countries have reading rooms where you can consult their newspapers.

● On subscription. It is possible to have foreign newspapers posted to you on a daily basis, although the cost is high. This can be arranged through an agency such as Collets Subscription Service, Denington Estate, Wellingborough, Northamptonshire NN8 2QT. Tel: (01933) 224351.

Details of the main newspapers in various countries around the world are given in Chapters 4 and 5.

USING THE EMPLOYMENT SERVICE

The UK Employment Service
It is possible to use the UK Employment Service to get a job in both the UK and some other countries. These are countries which are members of the European Union: Austria, Belgium, Denmark, Ireland, Finland, France, Germany, Greece, Italy, Luxembourg, the Netherlands, Portugal, Spain and Sweden. Norway also participates.

For details of these jobs visit your local Job Centre and ask for details of any vacancies in voluntary work which are available through the **Overseas Placing Unit** or OPU. These are usually jobs that government-run employment services in other countries have had difficulty filling, so they have asked the services in other countries to try and fill them.

If no suitable vacancies are available then fill in a form ES13 at the Job Centre. When you do this your details will be held on file and you will be contacted if any suitable vacancies arise through the OPU within the next six months.

The main limitation with this system is that most of the jobs that become available are for qualified and experienced people who speak a foreign language. If you are not already qualified and experienced the chances of finding a job may be small.

Using the job centres in foreign countries
Every foreign country has a government-run employment service very much like our Job Centres and, in many cases, it is possible for those from the UK to use this service to get a job.

People from the UK are legally entitled to use state employment services in all the European Union countries. You have a right to be treated equally with nationals of that country. However, remember that many of the jobs offered by these services will require qualifications, experience and knowledge of a foreign language. There will also usually be a lot of competition from people who already live in that country.

To use the state employment service in other countries you must usually visit them in person. They do not usually deal with telephone calls or letters from abroad. Some useful contacts are given later in Chapters 4 and 5.

USING PRIVATE EMPLOYMENT AGENCIES

Employment agencies in the UK

One way of finding the job you want is to register with a privately run employment agency. They will take your details and try and find you a job with an employer who has notified them of a vacancy.

The main limitation of this method is that **most of the jobs handled are for qualified and experienced people. Employment agencies may not have many jobs suitable for school and college leavers**. Most of the jobs handled by agencies will be in the UK, although they do sometimes have jobs in other countries of the world too.

Details of employment agencies in your area can be found in your local *Yellow Pages* under the heading 'Employment Agencies and Consultants'. Details of many more agencies throughout the UK can be found in a book called the FRES Yearbook, which will be in many libraries.

Some employment agencies in the UK:

Charity Appointments, 3 Spital Yard, London E1 6AQ. Tel: (020) 7247 4502. (Executive positions only.)

Charity People, The Chandlery, Westminster Bridge Road, London SE1 7QY. Tel: (020) 7721 7585.

Charity Recruitment, 40 Rosebery Avenue, London EC1R 4RN. Tel: (020) 7833 0414.

Employment agencies in the UK are not allowed to charge the employee a fee. This may not apply in other countries.

Using employment agencies in other countries

If you want to work abroad you should consider using private employment agencies in your chosen country. These are usually willing to help people from other countries, especially if you have a particular skill to offer and speak the local language.

Private employment agencies can be found in most foreign countries, although in a few (such as Germany) they are prohibited by law. Some useful contacts are given in Chapters 4 and 5.

The best way to find out if an employment agency may be able to help you is to put together a letter and CV (curriculum vitae) telling them about yourself and what you can do and then send it to all the agencies you can find.

Voluntary service bureaux

In addition to the commercially run employment agencies there are

voluntary service bureaux in many countries. These bureaux sometimes operate charitable projects of their own, but they also work to assist and advise voluntary agencies. This includes finding suitable employees for those voluntary agencies. For example, in the UK there is **Voluntary Service Overseas** (VSO). VSO does not run its own projects but specialises in recruiting experienced people for development projects run by other agencies, such as African governments or charities.

Details of some voluntary service bureaux in the UK and worldwide are given in Chapters 4 and 5. Details of voluntary service bureaux in other countries can usually be obtained from the embassy of the relevant country.

The best way to find out if a voluntary service bureau may be able to help you is to put together a letter and CV (curriculum vitae) telling them about yourself and what you can do and then post it off to all the agencies you can find.

GETTING A JOB BY DIRECT APPLICATION

A large number of voluntary work jobs are not found by actually looking for vacancies that are advertised in newspapers, trade publications and through agencies. They are mostly found by what is known as **speculative application**. This means that you actually approach potential employers and offer your services, rather than wait for them to advertise. The chances of being offered a job by doing this are greater than many people realise.

Some voluntary agencies rarely advertise their vacancies for staff. Instead they wait for people to contact them, as they feel this proves that you are genuinely interested in the job.

If you want to use this method then prepare a letter which tells a would-be employer about yourself and what you feel you can offer them. Also put together a CV which gives your personal details, and details of your education and of any work experience you have had. Send these to all the employers you can find out about, who you feel will have jobs of the type you want.

Addresses of possible employers can be obtained from:

● The *Yellow Pages*. Directories for all the UK and many foreign countries are available in most major libraries.

● Foreign Embassies. The London Embassies of most foreign countries are sometimes able to supply contact addresses for voluntary agencies and government departments in their country.

- The *Europa World Year Book*: lists government departments and offices in every country of the world. Available at most major libraries.

- *The Henderson Top 1,000 Charities* (published annually by Hemmington Scott Publishing). Lists charities in the UK and provides extensive background information on them. Available at some major libraries.

- *The Voluntary Agencies Directory* (published biannually by NCVO Publications). Lists agencies in the UK. Available at major bookshops.

- Many of the main voluntary agencies in the UK and worldwide are listed later in this book.

Some examples of letters and CVs are given later in this chapter.

GETTING A JOB BY PERSONAL CALLING

The method discussed above can be a very effective way of finding out about jobs. However, in some situations it can be quicker and easier to actually contact possible employers by telephone or in person, rather than writing them a letter and hoping they will reply.

This method is particularly suitable if you are looking for unpaid short-term work abroad. Just contact suitable voluntary agencies and ask if they have any vacancies.

Firstly
You must first find out the cost of travelling to the particular country you want to work in, and of staying there, while you look for a job. In some countries food and accommodation is more expensive than in the UK. It is a good idea to buy a ticket for your return journey before you travel out so that you can easily return home if no work is available.

Secondly
You must find out if you need any permits or visas in order to travel to the country and look for work. This is covered in Chapters 1, 4 and 5 and you can also find out by asking the Embassy or Consulate of the relevant country. Addresses for these are given in Chapters 4 and 5.

Thirdly
Make a list of possible employers before you leave the UK. This can be done by using the sources listed in the previous section.

Finally

When you arrive abroad decide what you are going to do and say before you set out to see a potential employer. Take a copy of your CV and any qualifications you hold. As well as asking them for a job be sure to tell them what you think you can offer their agency.

SAMPLE LETTERS AND CV

The following pages give you examples of letters to prospective employers and of a CV.

Tips on presenting letters and CVs

- A CV must always be typed and should fit on one side of one piece of A4 paper only.

- Letters may be handwritten or typed. If you write make sure your writing is neat and readable.

- Use good quality white or blue writing paper and write in black or blue only. Do not write letters on lined paper, or in red ink or pencil.

- Never send out a letter or CV containing any mistakes or any corrections.

- After you have written your letter and CV get a friend to read it through to make sure it is clear.

- Enclosing a stamped, self-addressed envelope with your letter will usually be appreciated when writing to a charity. (If writing abroad send International Reply Coupons or IRCs, which are obtainable at the post office. They can be exchanged for return postage stamps by the organisation you are writing to.)

GETTING THROUGH SELECTION AND INTERVIEW

- If your application is of interest you may be interviewed, possibly by a panel of two or three interviewers.

- Prepare for the interview carefully. Make sure you know exactly what the voluntary agency does and what its aims and objectives are.

The Manager,   John Black,
The Conservation Charity,   20 The Road,
Piccadilly,   Anytown,
London.   Lancashire LA1 1AA.
W1.   Tel: 0123 999999
                                                  1 April 200X

Dear Sir,

I am writing to introduce myself and enquire whether you might
have any vacancies for workers on the conservation projects which
you operate abroad.

I am 20 years old and currently work as an assistant in a local shop.
However, in the past I have successfully completed many
conservation projects in this area. Last summer I worked on a
project to create a nature reserve at a disused quarry. At the moment
I am working each weekend as part of a group which is reopening
the Anytown canal.

Having had experience on various projects I have now decided that
I would very much like to make a career in conservation work. I am
particularly interested in conservation projects in developing
countries, and I believe you have projects in Africa and South
America.

I enclose my CV which gives more details of my qualifications and
experience. If you have a job for which I might be suitable I would
be very interested to hear from you.

Yours faithfully,

John Black

Enclosed: CV.

Fig. 1. A letter to a possible employer
enquiring about suitable vacancies.

Ms Jacqueline Scott,   Jane Green,
Director,   30 The Road,
National Advice Bureaux,   Anytown,
Fleet Street.   Lancashire LA1 1AA.
London,   Tel: 0123 999999
EC1.   1 April 200X

Dear Ms Scott,

I would like to apply for the job of 'PR and Information Officer' as advertised in 'The Guardian' of 31 March 200X.

I am 30 years old and currently employed as a PR officer with a local company. My duties include providing a PR service and maintaining an information resource bank for members of the sales team. I also supervise the sales office.

In my spare time I am involved with voluntary work for two local voluntary organisations. These are the Anytown office of the Citizens Advice Bureaux, where I am a part time adviser, and our local branch of the RSPCA. I am the secretary for the branch and deal with all correspondence, minutes at meetings, and organisation of our annual fund raising events.

I have long been interested in making a career in the voluntary sector and now feel that my charity experience and business experience would prove very useful to an agency such as NAB. I have read your 'Aims and Commitments' booklet and fully understand and support them.

I enclose my curriculum vitae which gives some more details about myself. If you feel I would be suitable for this position then I would be very pleased to attend for an interview.

Yours sincerely,

Jane Green

Enclosed: CV.

Fig. 2. A letter applying for a job advertised by a voluntary agency.

CURRICULUM VITAE

Jane Green
30 The Road
Anytown
Lancashire LA1 1AA
Tel: 0123 999999

Born: 10 January 19XX, Manchester, XX years old.
Nationality: British
Status: Single

Education
June 19XX: A levels, English, French, Geography.
June 19XX: BSc Degree in Geography.

Work Experience
19XX–19XX
PR Assistant, Megamedia Plc. My duties included typing, filing, reception work, administration and basic PR duties.

19XX–19XX
PR Officer, Megamedia Plc. Providing a PR service for a variety of clients. This involved liaising with the press and TV, copywriting, press releases and speaking at meetings and conferences.

19XX–Present day
PR officer, JR Paints Ltd. JR Paints is a major paint manufacturer and distributor. I am in sole charge of the company's public relations activities and also provide support to the sales and marketing departments.

Outside Interests
Voluntary service for the Citizens Advice Bureau as an adviser.
Voluntary service for the RSPCA as branch secretary.
Travel: I have travelled extensively in France and Spain.
Sports: Tennis.

Other Information
I hold a full, clean driving licence.
I hold a St John Ambulance First Aid Certificate.
I speak a little French and Spanish.

Fig. 3. A sample CV.

Programme Manager, South Sudan

Based in Akot, South Sudan

2 year contract - Unaccompanied

OXFAM UK/I is seeking a Programme Manager to manage an integrated rehabilitation and relief programme, covering water, livestock and health activities, in eastern Bahr el Ghazal, southern Sudan.

Reporting to the Regional Representative who is based in Nairobi, you will be responsible for planning, co-ordinating and representing OXFAM's programme in the area, establishing effective management systems and managing programme staff.

You will need:

• at least 2 years relief and/or development experience with an NGO in Africa;

• proven analytical, management and organisational skills;

• experience of budgeting and financial controls;

• experience in one or more of the following areas: pastoralism, agriculture, water, health;

• knowledge of Arabic an advantage;

The ability to manage a team in an isolated and potentially stressful situation is also essential.

For further details and an application form, please send a large S.A.E. to the Overseas Personnel & Development Department quoting the reference OS/PC/SUD/AD.

Closing date: 3rd February

Interview date: 15th February

OXFAM UK/I, 274 Banbury Road, Oxford, OX2 7DZ

Working for a Fairer World

OXFAM UK/I IS STRIVING TO BE AN EQUAL OPPORTUNITY EMPLOYER

OXFAM UK/I works with poor people in their struggle against hunger, diseases, exploitation and poverty in Africa, Asia, Latin America and the Middle East through relief, development, research and public education

---

DISABILITY INFORMATION SERVICE
DISABILITY INFORMATION WORKER

30 hours per week LA SCP 22 £12,624 (pro rata)

A person with organisational and communication skills and with a commitment to raising the profile of disability issues, is needed to establish and develop this new project

Application form and further details from:

Paddy Mayes, Citizens Advice Bureau, 101 Station Parade, Harrogate HG1 1HB Telephone (0423) 560840

Closing date, February 4. Interviews, February 21

Working towards equal opportunities

52781   131 AH 3

ADVICE THAT MAKES A DIFFERENCE

□ Bureau Manager

citizens advice bureau

Local Authority Scale SO1

Starting salary £15,903

WINSFORD

37 hours per week

Busy town centre bureau requires a Manager to lead and develop a small team of paid specialists and volunteer advisers. The successful candidate will have proven team-management ability, excellent communication skills, and a commitment to equal opportunities.

For further details and an application form, write to: The Chair, Vale Royal District CABx, 48 Chesterway, Northwich, CW9 5JA. Mark the envelope "Job Application".

Closing date for applications: 28th January

Interview date: 23rd February

Working for Equal Opportunities

• CONFIDENTIAL • IMPARTIAL • INDEPENDENT • FREE •

Fig. 4. Sample job advertisements.

65

VOLUNTARY WORK SCHEME
APPLICATION
FORM

Please return to: Miss June Morse
Personnel Secretary
The Leonard Cheshire Foundation
26-29 Maunsel Street
London SW1P 2QN, U.K.

BLOCK CAPITALS PLEASE

SURNAME:_____ FIRST NAMES:_____

MALE/FEMALE:_____ DATE OF BIRTH: _____

ADDRESS: _____

_____

_____

COUNTRY: _____ NATIONALITY:_____

TELEPHONE: _____ DRIVING LICENCE: YES/NO*

QUALIFICATIONS (if any): _____

_____

WORKING AND/OR VOLUNTARY EXPERIENCE (if any): _____

_____

WHY DO YOU WANT TO DO THIS TYPE OF VOLUNTARY WORK?: _____

HAVE YOU ANY HEALTH PROBLEMS/DISABILITIES?: YES/NO*
IF YES, PLEASE GIVE BRIEF DETAILS:_____

_____

FOR WHAT PERIOD ARE YOU AVAILABLE? (Please give exact dates):
FROM: _____TO:_____

WHAT IS THE SHORTEST PERIOD OF NOTICE YOU WOULD NEED BEFORE THE DATE OF STARTING
WORK?:_____

ACCOMMODATION IS VERY LIMITED IN SOME HOMES. IF NO SINGLE ROOMS IS AVAILABLE ARE
YOU WILLING TO SHARE?   YES/NO*

* DELETE AS APPROPRIATE

Fig. 5. Sample application forms.

AREA   ARE PREPARED TO GO ANYWHERE IN THE U.K.?   YES/NO*

IF YOU ANSWER "NO" PLEASE STATE

What is your preferred area(s)?: _____

Do you wish to go only to the area given above, or if we cannot find you a suitable vacancy in that area do you wish to be notified of possibilities elsewhere?

PREFERRED AREA ONLY/WOULD CONSIDER ELSEWHERE*

LANGUAGE   If not British, have you a working knowledge of the English language? (This is _essential._ Volunteers **must** be able to understand clearly instructions about the care of our disabled residents - misunderstandings can be very dangerous.)   YES/NO*

How long have you been learning English?_____years

TYPE OF WORK   Nearly all our vacancies are in Homes for physically disabled adults. However, there are _very_ occasional opportunities for other types of work, which we appreciate that not all applicants would wish to consider. Please, therefore, tick yes or no below to show in which of the following types of job you would be interested, if available.

	YES	NO
Work in a Home for physically disabled adults		
Work in a Home for mentally handicapped adults		
Work in a Home for ex-psychiatric rehabilitation		
Work with a physically handicapped individual (or couple) living independently		

REFERENCES   Please give below the names and addresses of two responsible people from whom references may be obtained if required. These must _not_ be relatives. _Previous employers should be given as references where possible._ Forms returned without two names and addresses _will not be accepted._

NAME _____   NAME _____

ADDRESS_____   ADDRESS_____

_____   _____

_____   _____

Tel. No.:_____   Tel. No.:_____

Where did you hear about our Voluntary Work Scheme? _____

_____

Date:_____ Signed:_____

* DELETE AS APPROPRIATE

Fig. 5. Continued.

TOC H U.K. PROJECT APPLICATION FORM
(PLEASE USE BLOCK CAPITALS - BLACK PEN OR TYPE)

Surname .... Name Usually Known By ....

First Names ....

Date of Birth .... Age ....Female/Male

Permanent Address ....

....Post Code ....

Telephone(day)... (evening) ....

Temporary Address ....

....Post Code ....

Telephone(day).. (evening) ....

Dates at temporary address - FROM .... TO................................

Emergency Contact - Name & Relationship...

Address ....

.... Post Code .... Tel ....

ENTER NO. OF PROJECT CHOICES IN ORDER OF PREFERENCE:

       [1]   [2]   [3]   [4]   [5]

Have you previously been Police Computer Vetted for Toc H Projects?   Yes/No

If 'YES', enter date of clearance ....

If 'NO', have you ever been previously Police Computer Vetted?   Yes/No

If 'YES', enter date ....and send copy of clearance document or

enter name and address of organisation which carried this out:

....

....

Do you have a driving licence?   Yes/No

If 'YES', have you any endorsements? Please give details:

Have you experience of driving a mini bus?   Yes/No

Would you drive a mini bus on the project? - SEE NOTE 10   Yes/No

Is this part of your Duke of Edinburgh Award? - SEE NOTE 12   Yes/No

Do you wish to bring a child/children with you?   Yes/No

Fig. 5. Continued.

Where, or how, did you obtain this project booklet?

....

The following information helps Toc H to know if it is achieving a wide mixture of volunteers - please underline one of the following:

STATUS -   Employed   ETHNIC ORIGIN -   Arab
              Unemployed   Asian - Pakistani
              Retired   Bangladeshi
              Student - School   Chinese
                       College   Black - Afro-Caribbean
                       University   African
                                            White - European
Other: Please specify.....................................   Non-European

                                 Other: Please specify.......................................

*I ENCLOSE £5 REGISTRATION FEE

*I ENCLOSE £1 TOWARD THE REGISTRATION FEE - BEING ON A LOW INCOME - AND UNDERTAKE TO FORWARD THE REMAINING £4 DURING THE NEXT 3 WEEKS

*[*Delete whichever is not applicable]*

Signed ....Date...

TOC H
1 Forest Close
Wendover, Aylesbury
Bucks HP22 6BT

JAB/02.92(Rev)

Fig. 5. Continued.

TOC H - THE PROTECTION OF CHILDREN AND OTHERS

This form MUST BE SIGNED ANNUALLY by those participating in short-term residential projects in which Toc H has some responsibility for the care of any other person, and through which he or she may have private or unsupervised access to them.

**ALL THREE SECTIONS OF THE FORM MUST BE COMPLETED
AND IN BLOCK CAPITALS THROUGHOUT, PLEASE**

SECTION 1 - VOLUNTEER: I..

....(full name)

of ....

....(post code) ....
declare that I have never at any time been convicted of any sexual offence or any offence against children or young persons (i.e. those under 18 years).

Signed ....Date ....

NOTE: This work is exempt from the provisions of the Rehabilitation of Offenders Act 1974, by virtue of the Rehabilitation of Offenders Act 1974 (Exemptions) Order 1975. Volunteers are therefore not entitled to withhold information about convictions which for other purposes are 'spent' under the provisions of the Act.

SECTION 2 - REFERENCE: To be completed by a person who is currently a magistrate, doctor, head teacher, head of year, college principal, minister of religion, lawyer, probation officer, full-time social worker, or the authorised representative of a current employer for whom the above named has worked for AT LEAST 2 YEARS. This form must NOT be signed by a person who is a member of Toc H or a paid member of Toc H staff.

I ....(full name)

of ....

....(post code) ....

Tel ....Office or Title ....

....
certify that to the best of my knowledge and belief the person named on this form has no criminal record in the two areas listed.

Signed ....Date ....

Fig. 5. Continued.

70

SECTION 3 - PERSONAL REFERENCE: This reference must be signed by an adult, WHO IS NOT A MEMBER OF YOUR FAMILY, and who has known you personally for AT LEAST 2 YEARS and is willing to testify as to your suitability for the work described.* It may be completed by the same referee as overleaf. If a different referee signs, then full details of name, address, telephone number and occupation must be given.

*Different rules apply to those resident in a Home Office Institution e.g. Probation Hostel, YOI or prison - details from Toc H Headquarters.

I have read the description of the project(s) applied for and I testify that to the best of my knowledge and belief there is no reason to suggest that the person named on this form is not suitable for the work.

I have known..(NAME)for ....years

FULL NAME ....

Signed ....Date ....

of ....

....(post code) ....

Occupation ....Tel ....

JAJ/JAB/06.92(Rev)

Fig. 5. Continued.

71

VOLUNTEER EXCHANGE FORM

(PLEASE PRINT CLEARLY AND ANSWER ALL QUESTIONS)

1. First Name & Surname: _____   ☐ Male   ☐ Female

   Present Address: _____   Permanent Address: _____

   _____   _____

   _____   _____

   Telephone: _____   Telephone: _____

   Dates at this address: From: _____   To: _____

2. Birthdate: _____   Birthplace*: _____   3. EMERGENCY CONTACT

   Nationality: _____   Passport No.*: _____   Name: _____

   Occupation: _____   Telephone: _____
   (*If visa is required)

   5. REMARKS ON HEALTH/SPECIAL NEEDS

4. LANGUAGES   _____

   Speak well: _____   _____

   Speak some: _____   _____

   Understand: _____

6. PAST VOLUNTEER EXPERIENCES   7. GENERAL SKILLS
   (Indicate the country, year, and type of work)
   _____   _____

Fig. 5. Continued.

72

8. WORKCAMP CHOICES ACCORDING TO PREFERENCE

CODE	NAME	DATES	CODE	NAME	DATES
1.			4.		
2.			5.		
3.			6.		

9. BOOK ANOTHER CAMP FOR ME IF ALL ABOVE ARE FULL: ☐ YES ☐ NO

Dates available: _____ Country/region preferred: _____

TYPE OF PROJECT MOST PREFERRED *(Please number according to preference)*

☐ Archaeology   ☐ Renovation   ☐ Construction   ☐ Environmental   ☐ Physically disabled   ☐ Teenage camps

☐ Agriculture   ☐ Children   ☐ Elderly   ☐ Mentally disabled   ☐ Cultural/arts   ☐ Study camps

10. WHY DO YOU WISH TO TAKE PART IN A VOLUNTEER PROJECT? _____

I accept the conditions of participation according to the programme of this organization:

_____   _____
Sending Organization   Date

UNITED NATIONS ASSOCIATION (WALES)
INTERNATIONAL YOUTH SERVICE
TEMPLE OF PEACE, CATHAYS PARK, CARDIFF CF1 3AP.
TEL: (0222) 223088. FAX: 66557

_____
Signature
(Signature of parent if you are under 18)

© Alliance of European Voluntary Service Organizations

Fig. 5. Continued.

73

THE ROYAL SOCIETY FOR THE PROTECTION OF BIRDS

THE LODGE · SANDY · BEDFORDSHIRE · SG19 2DL · TEL: 0767 680551 · TELEX: 82469 RSPB · FAX: 0767 692365

| VOLUNTARY WARDENING SCHEME |

| A P P L I C A T I O N   F O R M |

Thank you for applying to take part in the Voluntary Wardening Scheme.
Please complete the information requested on __all sides__ of this form and I
will do my best to make a reservation for you. Details of our nature
reserves in the Scheme are given in the Information Leaflet enclosed.

HAVE YOU TAKEN PART IN THIS SCHEME BEFORE   YES ☐   NO ☐

TITLE : Mr/Mrs/Miss/Ms ....

FULL NAME: ....

ADDRESS: ....

....

POSTCODE: ....

TEL NO: HOME .... WORK ....

FAX NO: ....

DOB: ....

MALE ☐   FEMALE ☐

ARE YOU A RSPB MEMBER ☐ or NON-MEMBER ☐

IF A MEMBER OF RSPB PLEASE GIVE MEMBERSHIP NO...........................

Fig. 5. Continued.

OCCUPATION (please give brief description of duties or studies if student):

....
....
....
....
....
....

SPECIFIC SKILLS

....
....
....

HOBBIES:

....
....
....
....

ORNITHOLOGICAL EXPERIENCE: GOOD [ ] COMPETENT [ ] BEGINNER [ ] NONE [ ]

WHAT DO YOU HOPE TO GAIN FROM PARTICIPATING IN THIS SCHEME? (eg, Duke of
Edinburgh Award Training, Working Holiday, Work Experience, etc)

....
....
....

HAVE YOU TAKEN PART IN ANY SIMILAR SCHEMES? Please Give Brief Description

....
....
....
....
....

Fig. 5. Continued.

HOW WILL YOU GET TO THE RESERVE? - public transport/vehicle!

....

WILL YOU HAVE A VEHICLE AT THE RESERVE DURING YOUR STAY AND WHAT WILL IT BE? (eg, bicycle, car, van, etc)

....

PLEASE GIVE A CHOICE OF DATES (Saturday to Saturday only):

FIRST CHOICE ....

SECOND CHOICE ....

THIRD CHOICE ....

FOURTH CHOICE ....

FIFTH CHOICE ....

PLEASE INDICATE YOUR CHOICE OF RESERVES FROM THE LIST:

FIRST CHOICE ....

SECOND CHOICE ....

THIRD CHOICE ....

FOURTH CHOICE ....

FIFTH CHOICE ....

IF THESE CHOICES ARE NOT AVAILABLE WOULD YOU BE PREPARED TO BE PLACED AT A RESERVE IN A PARTICULAR REGION?

YES [ ]   NO [ ]

PLEASE INDICATE WHICH REGION YOU WOULD PREFER TO WORK IN (eg, Scotland, Wales, North England, East Anglia, South England):

....

WOULD YOU BE PREPARED TO WORK AT A RESERVE ANYWHERE ELSE ON A NATIONAL SCALE?

YES [ ]   NO [ ]

Fig. 5. Continued.

PLEASE INDICATE THAT YOU AGREE TO THE FOLLOWING BY SIGNING BELOW:

Accommodation is provided free at or near to the reserve but it will be necessary for you to pay your own travel expenses to get to the reserve and provide your own food during your stay.

Duties vary but range from physical management work, helping visitors and survey work, and will be allocated to you by the Reserve Warden according to your knowledge and experience.

Any observations made during your stay may only be published with prior permission of the RSPB.

SIGNED .... *DATE* ....

PLEASE RETURN YOUR APPLICATION FORM WITH A STAMPED ADDRESSED ENVELOPE TO:

Sandra Manners, Reserves Management Department, RSPB, The Lodge, Sandy, Bedfordshire. SG19 2DL

FOR OFFICE USE ONLY

APPLICATION RECEIVED .... *REPLY SENT* ....

Fig. 5. Continued.

BRITISH C.M.P. INTERNATIONAL WORKCAMPS 1993
APPLICATION FORM

Please use black ink and print clearly.

FIRST NAME................................ SURNAME.. SEX.........AGE.......

OCCUPATION OR STUDY SUBJECTS...

LANGUAGES: fluently spoken...a little...................................

PERMANENT ADDRESS: ....

....TEL ....

TEMPORARY ADDRESS: . ...

....TEL ....

DATES AT THIS ADDRESS: from ....1993 to.............................

CONTACT IN CASE OF EMERGENCY: ....

....TEL ....

PROJECT CHOICES

Choice	Code	Place	Dates	Code	Place	Dates
				(If you wish to string two projects together)		
1				and		
2				and		
3				and		
4				and		

I am willing to accept a place in any project organised in one of the countries stated above providing it takes place between the dates when I am free: YES/NO   Dates Free:

Any specific reasons for your choice ....

Previous voluntary work ....

How did you hear about the Christian Movement for Peace? ....

Any special needs?................................. ....

ORIENTATION WEEKEND.

Please reserve a space for me on the WOCC East/West Orientation day: YES/NO

Please reserve a space for me on the Middle East Orientation weekend: YES/NO

Please ensure that you have understood and followed our application procedure correctly with all enclosures (see page 3) and have enclosed a cheque (£40 per workcamp for non members, £35 for members).

Signed.. Date..

Signature of parent/guardian if under 18: . ...

Return as soon as possible to: *Project Applications, CMP, 186 St Paul's Road,*
Balsall Heath, Birmingham B12 8LZ

Office use only:	1:Ref No:	2:Appl chq rec :	3:Appl ackd
4:To 1st Choice:	5:Appl informed	Or to 2nd Choice:	3rd Choice
4th Choice	6:Cheque £	7:Actual Fee £	8:Refund £

Fig. 5. Continued.

- You may be tested. This applies if you have a specialist skill, such as medical skills, or knowledge of a foreign language.

- It may help if you can produce references or testimonials to prove that you are genuinely interested in voluntary work. Ask the project leaders of any voluntary projects you have already completed if they will give you these.

- You may have to be vetted to make sure you have no criminal record and make sure you have the qualifications and experience you have stated.

- You may have to attend an orientation meeting or selection course at which you meet other applicants and look more closely at the work of the agency.

4
Guide to Voluntary Work: Europe

EUROPEAN UNION AND SCANDINAVIA

The United Kingdom

About voluntary work in the UK

The number of voluntary agencies in the UK has grown steadily in recent years. There are now over 182,000 registered charities, providing a range of services which either add to services provided by the government, or stand in for these where they do not exist. Today the voluntary sector in the UK can be considered something of an industry; many agencies are well funded and very efficiently organised. Some agencies receive public money; others do not.

A voluntary agency can be considered as any organisation which provides a service for a reason other than profit. It could be:

● A registered charity.
● A club or society.
● An informal group of people with a common interest.
● A private company.
● An agency operated by a local authority.

In other words, not all voluntary agencies are charities. Most voluntary agencies operate at only one of four levels:

● Internationally: anywhere in the world.
● Nationally: anywhere in the UK.
● Regionally: only within your country or region.
● Locally: only within your town, or even just a part of it.

As a result it is important to choose the right voluntary agency according to the area in which you wish to work. Most voluntary agencies tend to concentrate their work on city areas, although there is often a need in rural areas and this is a growing area of voluntary work.

Voluntary agencies range in size from the very large to the very small. The largest charities in the UK employ around 1,500 people (although only a handful employ more than 300 or so); the smallest just one or two.

It is important to note that not all voluntary agencies use full-time paid volunteers, although this trend is increasing with the aim to be more efficient and professional. Very few voluntary agencies have organised recruitment systems and regular recruitment intakes. Often it is a matter of waiting for full-time vacancies to arise. And, when they do, people who have experience in similar but unpaid voluntary work tend to have an advantage at interview.

Career prospects with most UK voluntary agencies are quite good, with most agencies aiming to increase their size and range of services as funding allows. At their best, wages and conditions of service compare well with any commercial business and senior management and director positions are often open to those who have worked their way up from project worker or unpaid volunteer.

A final point to note about taking full-time voluntary work is that a number of posts are often open to job share: that is, working around 20 hours per week with a partner working the remaining time to the equivalent of one full-time job. Also, a number of positions are for fixed contracts, and only last so long as government, local authority, or donation funding lasts.

Types of work available
All types, as discussed in Chapter 2.

Sources to use
All methods, as discussed in Chapter 3.

Useful contacts
Some voluntary agencies:
Abbeyfield Society, 186-192 Darkes Lane, Potters Bar, Hertfordshire EN6 1AB. Tel: (01707) 44845. Provides small-scale residential homes for the elderly.

Action Against Allergy, 24-26 High Street, Hampton Hill, Middlesex TW12 1PD. Provides information on allergy, campaigns for, and raises funds for research.

Action & Research for Multiple Sclerosis (ARMS), 4a Chapel Hill, Stansted, Essex CM24 8AG. Tel: (01279) 815553.

Action for Benefits, 124 Southwark Street, London SE1 0TU. Tel: (020) 7928 9671. Campaigns for an improved welfare benefits system.

Action for Blind People, 14 Verney Road, London SE16 3DZ. Tel: (020) 7732 8771.

Action For Children (NCH), 85 Highbury Park, London N5 1UD. Tel: (020) 7226 2033. Operates homes and works on a variety of community projects.

Action for Sick Children, Argyle House, Euston Road, London NW1 2SD. Tel: (020) 7833 2041.

Action on Smoking and Health (ASH), 109 Gloucester Place, London W1H 3PH. Tel: (020) 7935 3519.

Action Aid, Hamlyn House, London N19 5PG. Tel: (020) 7281 4101. Works to provide self-help for poor families worldwide.

Advice Services Alliance (ASA), 88-94 Wentworth Street, London E1 7SA. Tel: (020) 7377 2538. Works to develop and improve the range of advice services on offer in the UK.

Advisory Council on Alcohol and Drug Education (TACADE), 1 Hulme Place, Salford, Manchester M5 4QA. Tel: (0161) 745 8925. Operates a drug and alcohol education and information service.

Africa Now, Bovis House, Townmead Road, London SW6 2RH. Tel: (020) 7371 5603. Provides help and finance to small communities in Africa.

Afro-Caribbean Education Resource Centre, Wyvil Road, London SW8 2TJ. Tel: (020) 7627 2662.

Age Concern, 1268 London Road, London SW16 4ER. Tel: (020) 8679 8000. Works to improve conditions for older people and their carers.

Aid for India, 186 Cowley Road, Oxford OX4 1UE. Tel: (01865) 728794.

AIDS Care Education and Training, PO Box 1323, London W5 5TF. Tel: (020) 8840 7879. A Christian charity providing home care to those with AIDS.

AIDS Education and Research Trust (AVERT), 11 Denne Parade, Horsham, West Sussex RH12 1JD. Tel: (01403) 210202.

Al-Anon Family Groups, 61 Great Dover Street, London SE1 4YF. Tel: (020) 7403 0888. Works to assist the families of alcoholics. Also incorporates Alateen, for teenage family members.

Alcohol Concern, 275 Gray's Inn Road, London WC1X 8QF. Tel: (020) 7833 3471. Works with other organisations to publicise the problems of alcohol abuse and obtain better treatment facilities.

Alcoholics Anonymous (AA), PO Box 1, The Stonebow, York YO1 2NJ. Tel: (01904) 644026.

Alone in London Service (ALS), West Lodge, 190 Euston Road, London NW1 2EF. Tel: (020) 7387 6184. Works to assist single homeless people in London by providing advice and accommodation.

Alzheimer's Disease Society, Gordon House, 10 Greencoat Place, London SW1P. Tel: (020) 7306 0606.

Amnesia Association, 7 King Edward Court, Nottingham NG1 1EW. Tel: (0115) 924 0800.

Amnesty International British Section, 99-119 Rosebery Avenue, London EC1R 4RE. Tel: (020) 814 6200. Works for the release of those imprisoned worldwide because of their sex, colour, race or beliefs.

Anchor Housing Trust, 269a Banbury Road, Oxford OX2 7HU. Tel: (01865) 311511. Provides housing and care for elderly people.

Anorexia and Bulimia Nervosa Association, Tottenham Town Hall, London N15 4RB. Tel: (020) 8885 3936.

Apex Trust, 2-4 Colchester Street, London E1 7TG. Tel: (020) 7481 4831. Works to improve the situation for those with a criminal record.

Army Benevolent Fund, 41 Queens Gate, London SW7 5HR. Tel: (020) 7581 8684.

Arthritis Care, 18 Stephenson Way, London NW1 2HD. Tel: (020) 7916 1500.

Asian Young Women's Project, 8 Manor Gardens, London N7 6JZ. Tel: (020) 7263 6270.

Association for Nonsmokers' Rights, Melgund Terrace, Edinburgh EH7 4BU. Tel: (0131) 557 3139.

Association for Self-Help and Community Groups, 14 Hillfield Park, London N10 3QS. Tel: (020) 8444 8664. Works to develop skills required to successfully run groups.

Association for Spina Bifida and Hydrocephalus, 42 Park Road, Peterborough PE1 2UQ. Tel: (01733) 555988.

Association of Charitable Foundations (ACF), 52 High Holborn, London WC1V 6RL. Tel: (020) 7404 1338.

Association of Community Workers in the UK, Stephenson Building, Elswick Road, Newcastle Upon Tyne NE4 6SQ. Tel: (0191) 272 4341.

ATD Fourth World, 48 Addington Street, London SE5 7LB. Tel: (020) 7703 3231. An international movement with a presence in many countries which works to eliminate poverty.

BAM (Freres des Hommes UK), 8 St Michael's Road, London SW9 0SL. An international movement with a presence in many countries which works on self-help projects.

Bankruptcy Association, 4 Johnson Close, Lancaster LA1 5EU. Tel: (01524) 64305. Provides support and advice to debtors and those facing bankruptcy; campaigns for changes in the bankruptcy laws.

Barnardo's, Tanners Lane, Barkingside, Ilford, Essex IG6 1QG. Children's charity providing support to a wide range of young people and their families. Operates homes and day centres and also works in the community. Tel: (020) 8550 8822.

Birth Control Trust, 27-35 Mortimer Street, London W1N 7RJ. Tel: (020) 7580 9360.

Birthright, 27 Sussex Place, London NW1 4SP. Tel: (020) 7262 5337. Funds medical research into the health of women and babies.

Blue Cross, Shilton Road, Burford, Oxfordshire OX18 4PF. Tel: (01993) 822651. Animal charity providing veterinary care and animal homes.

Breast Cancer Research Trust, 104 Harley Street, London W1N 4AJ. Tel: (020) 7435 7731.

British Association of the Hard of Hearing, 7-11 Armstrong Road, London W3 7JL. Tel: (020) 7734 1110.

British Council of Organisations of Disabled People (BCODP), De Bradelei House, Chapel Street, Belper, Derbyshire DE56 1AR. Tel: (01773) 828182.

British Deaf Association, 38 Victoria Place, Carlisle CA1 1HU. Tel: (01228) 48844.

British Diabetic Association (BDA), 10 Queen Anne Street, London W1M 0BD. Tel: (020) 7323 1531.

British Epilepsy Association, 40 Hanover Square, Leeds LS3 1BE. Tel: (0113) 243 9393.

British Heart Foundation, 14 Fitzhardinge Street, London W1H 4DH. Tel: (020) 7935 0185.

British Kidney Patients' Association, Bordon, Hampshire GU35 9JP. Tel: (01420) 472021.

BLESMA – British Limbless Ex-Servicemen's Association, 185 High Road, Chadwell Heath, Essex RM6 6NA. Tel: (020) 8590 1124.

British Lung Foundation, 8 Peterborough Mews, London SW6 3BL. Tel: (020) 7371 7704.

British Organ Donor Society (BODY), Balsham, Cambridge CB1 6DL. Tel: (01223) 893636.

British Pregnancy Advisory Service, Austy Manor, Wootton Wawen, Solihull, W Midlands B95 6BX. Tel: (01564) 793225.

British Red Cross Society, 9 Grosvenor Crescent, London SW1X 7EJ. Tel: (020) 7235 5454. Provides both emergency and regular caring services of many different types anywhere in the UK or abroad (through the International Red Cross Movement).

British Sports Association for the Disabled, Solecast House, 13-27 Brunswick Place, London N1 6DX. Tel: (020) 7490 4919.

British Trust for Conservation Volunteers (BTCV), 36 St Mary's Street, Wallingford, Oxfordshire OX10 0EU. Tel: (01491) 39766. Publicises the cause of nature conservation and organises conservation projects.

British Union for the Abolition of Vivisection (BUAV), 16a Crane Grove, London N7 8LB. Tel: (020) 7700 4888.

Brook Advisory Centres, 153a East Street, London SE17 2SD. Tel: (020) 7708 1390. Operates advice services for young people on sex and contraception.

CAFOD, Romero Close, Stockwell Road, London SW9 9TY. Tel: (020) 7733 7900. Catholic charity working on relief and development projects in over 75 countries.

Campaign for Freedom of Information, 88 Old Street, London EC1V 9AR. Tel: (020) 7253 2445.

Campaign for Homosexual Equality, PO Box 342, London WC1X 0DU. Tel: (020) 7833 3912.

Campaign for Nuclear Disarmament (CND), 162 Holloway Road, London N7 8DQ. Tel: (020) 7700 2393.

Campaign for Press and Broadcasting Freedom, 96 Dalston Lane, London E8 1NG. Tel: (020) 7923 3671.

Cancer Relief Macmillan Fund, Anchor House, 15-19 Britten Street, London SW3 2TZ. Tel: (020) 7351 7811. Provides care for those suffering from cancer by way of Macmillan nurses and Macmillan centres.

Cancer Research Campaign, 6-10 Cambridge Terrace, London NW1Y 4JL. Tel: (020) 7224 1333.

Care, 36-38 Southampton Street, London WC2E 7HE. Tel: (020) 7379 5247. Works on projects in developing countries.

Catholic AIDS Link, PO Box 646, London E9 6QP. Tel: (020) 8986 0807.

Centrepoint Soho, Gloucester Mansions, Cambridge Circus, London WC2H 8HD. Tel: (020) 7379 3466. Works against homelessness and provides accommodation for young homeless people.

CHAR – Housing Campaign for Single People, 5 Cromer Street, London WC1H 8LS. Tel: (020) 7833 2071.

Child Poverty Action Group (CPAG), 1-5 Bath Street, 4th Floor, London EC1V 9PY. Tel: (020) 7253 3406. Researches into poverty, publicises the problems and provides an advice service on welfare benefits.

ChildLine, Royal Mail Building, Studd Street, London N1 0QW. Tel: (020) 7239 1000. Provides a helpline service for children.

Christian Aid, Interchurch House, 35 Lower Marsh, London SE1 7RL. Tel: (020) 7620 4444. Works on disaster relief and development worldwide.

Christians Abroad, 1 Stockwell Green, London SW9 9HP. Tel: (020) 7737 7811. Provides information and support to Christians, and others, working abroad and/or returning from voluntary work abroad.

Church Army, Independents Road, London SE3 9LG. Tel: (020) 8318 1226. Operates hostels, youth centres, homes for the elderly and undertakes social work and prison visiting.

Community Service Volunteers, 237 Pentonville Road, London N1 9NJ. Tel: (020) 7278 6601. Sends young people on community projects, trains the unemployed and finds older people with skills/experience to help with voluntary projects.

Compassion in World Farming Trust, 5a Charles Street, Petersfield, Hampshire GU32 3EH. Tel: (01730) 264208. Campaigns for the abolition of factory farming.

Contact a Family, 170 Tottenham Court Road, London W1P 0HA. Tel: (020) 7383 3555. Supports families caring for children with special needs.

Co-operation for Development, 21 Germain Street, Chesham, Buckinghamshire HP5 1LB. Tel: (01494) 775557. Works against poverty in a variety of projects worldwide.

Coronary Prevention Group (CPG), 102 Gloucester Place, London W1H 3DA. Tel: (020) 7935 2889. Works to promote the cause of preventing heart disease.

Cot Death Society, 116 Alt Road, Formby, Liverpool L37 8BW. Tel: (01704) 870005.

Council for the Protection of Rural England (CPRE), Warwick House, Buckingham Palace Road, London SW1W 0PP. Tel: (020) 7976 6433. Works to protect the countryside, with research and lobbying.

CMP – The Christian Movement for Peace, 186 St Paul's Road, Birmingham B12 8LZ. Tel: (0121) 446 5704. Operates community service projects in various parts of Europe.

Cruse Bereavement Care, 126 Sheen Road, Richmond, Surrey TW9 1UR. Tel: (020) 8940 4818.

Cystic Fibrosis Research Trust, 5 Blyth Road, Bromley, Kent BR1 3RS. Tel: (020) 8464 7211.

Down's Syndrome Association, 153-155 Mitcham Road, London SW17 9PG. Tel: (020) 8682 4001.

Electoral Reform Society, 6 Chancel Street, London SE1 0UU. Tel: (020) 7928 1622. Works towards the introduction of proportional representation and studies/provides information on the electoral process.

Family Planning Association, 27-33 Mortimer Street, London W1N 7RJ. Tel: (020) 7636 7866.

Foundation for the Study of Infant Deaths, 35 Belgrave Square, London SW1X 8QB. Tel: (020) 7235 0965.

Friends of the Earth, 26-28 Underwood Street, London N1 7JQ. Tel: (020) 7490 1555. Campaigns for the protection of the environment.

Fullemploy Group Ltd, 91 Brick Lane, London E1 6ZN. Tel: (020) 7827 9090. Works for racial equality and provides training for the unemployed.

Gamblers Anonymous, PO Box 88, London SW10 0EU. Tel: (020) 8741 4181.

Gingerbread, 35 Wellington Street, London WC2E 7BN. Tel: (020) 7240 0953. Provides support for one-parent families.

Greenpeace, Canonbury Villas, London N1 2PN. Tel: (020) 7354 5100. Works to protect the environment.

Guide Dogs for the Blind Association, Hillfields, Burghfield Common, Berkshire RG7 3YG. Tel: (01189) 835555.

Help the Aged, St James Walk, London EC1R 0BE. Tel: (020) 7253 0253.

Homes for Homeless People, 90-92 Bromham Road, Bedford MK40 2QH. Tel: (01234) 350853. Supports groups around the country which work with homeless people.

Howard League for Penal Reform, 708 Holloway Road, London N19 3NL. Tel: (020) 7281 7722.

Imperial Cancer Research Fund, PO Box 123, London WC2A 3PX. Tel: (020) 7242 0200.

Infertility Advisory Centre Research Foundation, 15 Berkeley Street, London W1X 5AE. Tel: (020) 7224 4724.

Institute of Community Relations, 2 Amhurst Park, London N16 5AE. Tel: (020) 8800 8612. Promotes relations between Orthodox Jews and other groups.

Intermediate Technology, Myson House, Railway Terrace, Rugby, Warwickshire CV21 3HT. Tel: (01788) 560631. Helps poor countries to develop in the way that is most appropriate for them, and not necessarily along the same lines as western countries.

International Rescue Corps (IRC), 8 Kings Road, Grangemouth, Stirling FK3 9BB. Tel: (01324) 665011. Provides rescue teams for disasters worldwide.

International Voluntary Service South (IVS), Old Hall, East Bergholt, Colchester CO7 6TQ. Tel: (01206) 298215.

IVS North, 188 Roundhay Road, Leeds LS8 5PL.

IVS Scotland, St Johns Church, Princes Street, Edinburgh EH2 4BJ.

Jewish Care, Stuart Young House, 221 Golders Green Road, London NW11 9DQ. Tel: (020) 8458 3382. Provides services for disabled and elderly people and their families.

King George's Fund for Sailors, 8 Hatherley Street, London SW1P 2YY. Tel: (020) 7932 0000.

Lantern Trust, 72 Honey Lane, Waltham Abbey, Essex EN9 3BS. Tel: (01992) 714900. Provides information on AIDS and promotes discussion and debate on the subject.

Law Centres Federation, Duchess House, 18-19 Warren Street, London W1P 5DB. Tel: (020) 7387 8570. Provides support for law centres around the country.

League Against Cruel Sports (LACS), 83 Union Street, London SE1 SG. Tel: (020) 7403 6155.

Leonard Cheshire Foundation, 26-29 Maunsel Street, London SW1P

2QN. Tel: (020) 7828 1822. Operates 270 Cheshire Homes worldwide accommodating disabled people.

Leukaemia Research Fund, 43 Great Ormond Street, London WC1N 3JJ. Tel: (020) 7405 0101.

Liberty – National Council for Civil Liberties, 21 Tabard Street, London SE1 4LA. Tel: (020) 7403 3888. Works to protect and extend the range of civil liberties available in the UK.

Local Authorities Race Relations Information Exchange, 81 Black Prince Road, London SE1 7SZ. Tel: (020) 7627 9628. Provides an information service on local authority race relations policy.

London Lighthouse, 111-117 Lancaster Road, London W11 1QT. Tel: (020) 7792 1200. Provides support for those affected by HIV and AIDS.

London Voluntary Service Council, 350 Holloway Road, London N19 1JB. Tel: (020) 7388 0241.

Low Pay Unit, 27 Amwell Street, London EC1R 1UN. Tel: (020) 7713 7581. Researches on, and publicises, the issues of poverty and low pay.

Marie Curie Cancer Care, 28 Belgrave Square, London SW1X 8QG. Tel: (020) 7235 3325.

Mental Aftercare Association, Bainbridge House, Bainbridge Street, London WC1A 1HP. Tel: (020) 7436 6194. Provides services for mentally disabled people living in the community.

Mental Health Foundation, 37 Mortimer Street, London W1N 7RJ. Tel: (020) 7580 0145.

Methodist Homes for the Aged, Stuart Street, Derby DE1 2EQ. Tel: (01332) 296200.

MIND – National Association for Mental Health, 22 Harley Street, London W1N 2ED. Tel: (020) 7637 0741. Works to protect the interests of those suffering from mental health problems.

Minority Rights Group, 379 Brixton Road, London SW9 7DE. Tel: (020) 7978 9498. Campaigns against discrimination and publicises instances of discrimination.

Motability, Gate House, West Gate, Harlow, Essex CM20 1HR. Tel: (01279) 635666. Operates schemes to provide cars and wheelchairs for disabled people.

Motor Neurone Disease Association, PO Box 246, Northampton NN1 2PR. Tel: (01604) 250505.

Multiple Sclerosis Society of Great Britain, 25 Effie Road, London SW6 1EE. Tel: (020) 7610 7171.

Muscular Dystrophy Group, 7 Prescott Place, London SW4 6BS. Tel: (020) 7720 8055.

National AIDS Trust, Euston Tower, Euston Road, London NW1 3DN. Tel: (020) 7383 4246.

NACRO – National Association for the Care and Resettlement of Offenders, 169 Clapham Road, London SW9 0PU. Tel: (020) 7582 6500.

National Association of Citizens Advice Bureaux (NACAB), 115-123 Pentonville Road, London N1 9LZ. Tel: (020) 7833 2181. Provides an advice service to the public through local Citizens Advice Bureaux.

National Association of Councils for Voluntary Service, Arundel Court, Arundel Street, Sheffield S1 2NU. Tel: (0114) 278 6636.

National Association of Hospital Broadcasting Organisations, 107 Bare Lane, Morecambe, Lancashire LA4 6RP. Tel: (01524) 415809.

National Association of Leagues of Hospital Friends, 2nd Floor, Fairfax House, Causton Road, Colchester, Essex CO1 1RJ.

National Association of Prison Visitors, 46b Hartington Street, Bedford MK41 7RL. Tel: (01234) 59763.

National Association of Volunteer Bureaux, St Peter's College, Saltley, Birmingham B8 3TE. Tel: (0121) 327 0265.

National Asthma Campaign, Providence House, Providence Place, London N1 0NT. Tel: (020) 7226 2260.

National Canine Defence League (NCDL), Pratt Mews, London NW1 0AD. Tel: (020) 7388 0137.

National Claimants Federation, PO Box 21, Plymouth PL1 1AB. Tel: (01793) 615773. Campaigns for improvements in the welfare benefits system.

National Council for One Parent Families, 255 Kentish Town Road, London NW5 2LX. Tel: (020) 7267 1361.

National Debtline, Birmingham Settlement, 318 Summer Lane, Birmingham B19 3RL. Tel: (0121) 359 8501. Provides advice to people with mortgage and rent arrears and other debts.

National Federation of Young Farmers' Clubs, YFC Centre, National Agriculture Centre, Kenilworth, Warwickshire CV8 2LG. Tel: (024) 76696544.

National League of the Blind and Disabled, Tenterden Road, London N17 8BE. Tel: (020) 8808 6030.

National Association for Epilepsy, Chalfont St Peter, Gerrards Cross, Buckinghamshire SL9 0RJ. Tel: (01494) 873991.

National Trust (National Trust for Places of Historic Interest and Beauty), 36 Queen Anne's Gate, London SW1H 9AS. Tel: (020) 7222 9251. It works to preserve buildings and land of particular historic interest or beauty.

NSPCC – National Society for the Prevention of Cruelty to Children, 67 Saffron Hill, London EC1N 8RS. Tel: (020) 7242 1626.

Noise Abatement Society, PO Box 8, Bromley, Kent BR2 0US. Tel: (020) 8460 3146. Campaigns to control noise pollution.

Ockenden Venture, Constitution Hill, Woking, Surrey GU22 7UU. Tel: (01483) 772012. Provides support to refugees on various projects both in the UK and abroad.

Oxfam, 274 Banbury Road, Oxford OX2 7DZ. Tel: (01865) 311311. Works on disaster relief, health, agricultural, educational and development projects in over 70 countries. Raises funds for this work in the UK, partly through a large network of charity shops.

Pax Christi, 9 Henry Road, London N4 2LH. Tel: (020) 8800 4612. A Catholic charity which works for peace in a variety of ways.

Peace Advertising Campaign, PO Box 24, Oxford OX1 3JZ. Tel: (01865) 722002. Works to keep the issues of world peace and disarmament in the public eye.

Peace Brigades International, 83 Margaret Street, London W1N 7HB. Tel: (020) 7636 5564. Provides peace observers in troublespots worldwide.

Peace Pledge Union, 6 Endsleigh Street, London WC1H 0LX. Tel: (020) 7387 5501. Works for peace, against war, and for non-violent ways of solving problems.

PDSA – People's Dispensary for Sick Animals, Whitechapel Way, Priorslee, Telford TF2 9PQ. Tel: (01952) 290999. Provides free veterinary care to pet owners who cannot afford to pay.

PHAB Ltd, Arkwright Centre, Irchester, Northants NN9 7EY. Tel: (01933) 412229. Runs clubs in which the physically handicapped and able-bodied can meet.

Piccadilly Advice Centre, 100 Shaftesbury Avenue, London W1V 7DH. Tel: (020) 7437 1579. Provides information on housing to young people in London.

Pregnancy Advisory Service, 11 Charlotte Street, London W1P 1HD. Tel: (020) 7637 8962.

Prince's Youth Business Trust, 5 Cleveland Place, London SW1Y 6JJ. Tel: (020) 7321 6500. Provides support and financial backing to young people who want to set up in business.

Prisoners Advice and Information Network, London WC1N 3XX. Tel: (020) 8542 3744.

Prisoners Wives and Families Association, 254 Caledonian Road, London N1 0NG. Tel: (020) 7278 3981.

QUIT – National Society of Non Smokers, 102 Gloucester Place, London W1H 3DA. Tel: (020) 7487 2858.

RADAR – Royal Association for Disability and Rehabilitation, 25 Mortimer Street, London W1N 8AB. Tel: (020) 7637 5400. It coordinates the work of more than 500 member organisations and campaigns on issues relevant to the disabled.

REACH, 89 Southwark Street, London SE1 0HD. Tel: (020) 7928 0452.

It links voluntary agencies with retired people having skills/experience to offer.

Relate, Herbert Gray College, Little Church Street, Rugby, Warwickshire CV21 3AP. Tel: (01788) 573241.

Returned Volunteer Action, 1 Amwell Street, London EC1R 1UL. Tel: (020) 7278 0804.

Riding for the Disabled, National Agricultural Centre, Kenilworth, Warwickshire CV8 2LY. Tel: (024) 7669 6510.

Royal British Legion, 48 Pall Mall, London SW1Y 5JY. Tel: (020) 7973 7200. Provides companionship and care for service personnel and ex-personnel. Undertakes fund raising, training and operates residential homes.

RNID – Royal National Institute for Deaf People, 105 Gower Street, London WC1E 6AH. Tel: (020) 7387 8033.

RNIB – Royal National Institute for the Blind, 224 Great Portland Street, London W1N 6AA. Tel: (020) 7388 1266.

RNLI – Royal National Lifeboat Institution, West Quay Road, Poole, Dorset BH15 1HZ. Tel: (01202) 671133.

Royal Society for Mentally Handicapped Children and Adults – MENCAP, 123 Golden Lane, London EC1Y 0Rt. Tel: (020) 7454 0454.

RSPCA – Royal Society for the Prevention of Cruelty to Animals, The Causeway, Horsham, Sussex RH12 1HG. Tel: (01403) 64181.

RSPB – Royal Society for the Protection of Birds, The Lodge, Sandy, Bedfordshire SG19 2DL. Tel: (01767) 680551.

Runnymede Trust, 11 Princelet Street, London E1 6QH. Tel: (020) 7375 1496. Works against racism and discrimination.

Salvation Army, 101 Queen Victoria Street, London EC4P 4EP. Tel: (020) 7236 5222. For social work: 105-109 Judd Street, London WC1H 9TS. Operates worldwide. Established to spread the Gospel but activities include providing homes and help for the old, young, disabled and homeless, community centres, clinics, community projects and disaster/emergency relief.

Samaritans, 10 The Grove, Slough, Berkshire SL1 1QP. Tel: (01753) 532713. The Samaritans offer a confidential befriending service through more than 180 branches in the UK.

Save the Children Fund, 17 Grove Lane, London SE5 8RD. Tel: (020) 7703 5400. It operates health, education, welfare and community projects in the UK and 30 other countries.

Sense – The National Deaf-Blind and Rubella Association, 11-13 Clifton Terrace, London N4 3SR. Tel: (020) 7272 7774. Works to improve knowledge of and services for the deaf-blind.

SHAC, 189a Old Brompton Road, London SW5 0AR. Tel: (020) 7373 7276. Provides advice on housing and related problems in London.

Shelter, 88 Old Street, London EC1V 9HU. Tel: (020) 7253 0202. Works towards the provision of affordable housing for everyone.

Simon Community, PO Box 1187, London NW5 9HW. Tel: (020) 7485 6639. Provides help to the homeless and campaigns for greater support for homeless people.

Skillshare Africa, 3 Belvoir Street, Leicester LE1 6SL. Tel: (0116) 2541862. Provides skilled and qualified people to work on development projects in Africa.

SSAFA – Soldiers', Sailors' and Airmen's Families Association, 19 Queen Elizabeth Street, London SE1 2LP. Tel: (020) 7403 8783. Provides welfare and advice services for service and ex-service personnel and their families.

SSPCA – Scottish Society for the Prevention of Cruelty to Animals, 19 Melville Street, Edinburgh, EH3 7PL. Tel: (0131) 225 6418.

Spastics Society, 12 Park Crescent, London W1N 4EQ. Tel: (020) 7636 5020.

Spinal Injuries Association, Newpoint House, St James's Lane, London N10 3DF. Tel: (020) 8444 2121.

St John Ambulance, 1 Grosvenor Crescent, London SW1X 7EF. Tel: (020) 7235 5231. Promotes public knowledge of first aid and provides first aid services to the community.

Students Nightline, National Co-ordinators, c/o Guild of Students, Birmingham University, Birmingham B15 2TU. Co-ordinates the services provided by nightlines at many UK universities.

Sue Ryder Foundation, Cavendish, Sudbury, Suffolk CO10 8AY. Tel: (01787) 280252. Provides support and residential homes for the sick and disabled.

Terrence Higgins Trust, 52-54 Gray's Inn Road, London WC1X 8JU. Tel: (020) 7831 0330. Provides support to people with AIDS, their families and friends, and generally publicises the situation.

Third World First (3W1), 217 Cowley Road, Oxford OX4 1XG. Tel: (01865) 245678. Works to raise awareness of third world issues.

TocH, 1 Forest Close, Wendover, Aylesbury, Bucks HP22 6BT. Tel: (01296) 623911. Operates a range of community projects, mostly involving work with young people.

UK Association of Rights and Humanity, 65a Swinton Street, London WC1X 9NT. Tel: (020) 7837 4188. It works to promote good community relations and advises people on their rights.

United Nations Association (Wales) International Youth Service, Temple of Peace, Cathays Park, Cardiff CF1 3AP. Tel: (029) 2022 3088. Recruits volunteers for community projects in the UK and abroad.

University of the Third Age (U3A), 1 Stockwell Green, London SW9 9JF.

Tel: (020) 7737 2541. Promotes education for retired people, including support of self-help groups.

Vegetarian Society of the United Kingdom, Parkdale, Dunham Road, Altrincham, Cheshire WA14 4QC. Tel: (0161) 298 0793.

Victim Support, Cranmer House, 39 Brixton Road, London SW9 6DZ. Tel: (020) 7735 9166. Provides advice and support to the victims of crime.

Voluntary Service Overseas, 317 Putney Bridge Road, London SW15 2PN. Tel: (020) 8780 2266. Recruits experienced and qualified people to work, for other agencies, on their development projects overseas.

War on Want, 37-39 Great Guildford Street, London SE1 0ES. Tel: (020) 7620 1111. Campaigns against poverty and supports development projects worldwide.

Water Aid, 1 Queen Anne's Gate, London SW1H 9BT. Tel: (020) 7233 4800. Provides support to third world communities in order to establish clean water supplies and sanitation.

Women's International League for Peace and Freedom, 157 Lyndhurst Road, Worthing, Sussex BN11 2DG. Tel: (01903) 295161. Works against discrimination and also for the advancement of peaceful relations between nations.

Women's Royal Voluntary Service (WRVS), 234-244 Stockwell Road, London SW9 9SP. Tel: (020) 7416 0146.

World Vision of Britain, Dynchurch House, 8 Abington Street, Northampton NN1 2AJ. Tel: (01604) 22964. A Christian aid and development organisation working in almost 100 countries worldwide.

World Wide Fund for Nature (WWF), Panda House, Weyside Park, Godalming, Surrey GU7 1XR. Tel: (01483) 426444. Raises funds for the conservation of rare animals and plants.

YMCA – Young Men's Christian Association, 640 Forest Road, London E17 3DZ. Tel: (020) 8520 5599. Provides housing, support, advice and social facilities for young people.

YWCA – Young Women's Christian Association of Great Britain, Clarendon House, 52 Cornmarket Street, Oxford OX1 3EJ. Tel: (01865) 726110. Provides housing, support, advice and social facilities for young people.

Voluntary Service Bureaux

Advance London, 14 Bloomsbury Square, London WC1X 1EP. Tel: (020) 7831 9873.

Bournemouth Voluntary Workers Bureau, 167 Holdenhurst Road, Bournemouth BH8 8DT. Tel: (01202) 293300.

Bristol Council for Voluntary Service, Beauley Road, Bristol BS3 1QC. Tel: (0117) 966 2676.

Clywd Voluntary Services, Station Road, Ruthin, Clwyd LL15 1BP. Tel: (01824) 707246.

Gwent Voluntary Bureau, 8 Pentonville Street, Newport, Gwent NP1 3PH. Tel: (01663) 213229.

Leicester Volunteers Bureau, 32 De Montfort Street, Leicester LE1 7GD. Tel: (0116) 255 3333.

Scottish Community Education Council, 2 Canning Street, Edinburgh EH3 8EG. Tel: (0131) 229 2433.

Other useful contacts

Association of Community Workers in the UK, Stephenson Buildings, Elswick Road, Newcastle Upon Tyne NE4 6SQ. Tel: (0191) 272 4341.

Charity Commission, Woodfield House, Tangier, Taunton, Somerset TA1 4BL. Tel: (01823) 345000.
  and
    57 Haymarket, London SW1Y 4QX. Tel: (020) 7210 4477.
    Graeme House, Derby Square, Liverpool L2 7SB. Tel: (0151) 227 3191.

Charities Aid Foundation, 48 Pembury Road, Tonbridge, Kent TN9 2JD. Tel: (01732) 771333.

Charities Advisory Trust, Radius Works, Back Lane, London NW3 1HL. Tel: (020) 7794 9835.

Charities Effectiveness Review Trust (CERT), 12 Mercer Street, London WC2H 9QE. Tel: (020) 7497 2499.

Charities Evaluation Services, 1 Motley Avenue, London EC2A 4SU. Tel: (020) 7613 1202.

Charity Forum, 60 Laurel Avenue, Potters Bar, Herts EN6 2AB. Tel: (01707) 662448.

Commission for Racial Equality, Elliot House, 10-12 Allington Street, London SW1E 5EH. Tel: (020) 7828 7022.

Council for Charitable Support, 48 Pembury Road, Tonbridge, Kent TN9 2JD. Tel: (01732) 771333.

Equal Opportunities Commission: Voluntary Organisations Liaison Unit, Overseas House, Quay Street, Manchester M3 3HN. Tel: (0161) 833 9244.

Home Office Voluntary Services Unit, Queen Anne's Gate, London SW1H 9AT. Tel: (020) 7273 2146.

National Council for Voluntary Organisations (NCVO), Regent's Wharf, 8 All Saints Street, London N1 9RL. Tel: (020) 7713 6161.

Northern Ireland Council for Voluntary Action, 127 Ormeau Road, Belfast BT7 1SH. Tel: (028) 9032 1224.

Overseas Development Administration (ODA), 94 Victoria Street, London SW1E 5JL. Tel: (020) 7393 1600.

and:

Abercrombie House, Eaglesham Road, East Kilbride, Glasgow G75
   8EA. Tel: (01355) 241199.
Scottish Council for Voluntary Organisations, 18 Claremont Crescent,
   Edinburgh EH7 4QD. Tel: (0131) 556 3882.
Wales Council for Voluntary Action, Llys Ifor, Crescent Road, Caerphilly
   CF8 1XL. Tel: (029) 2086 9224.

How to find out about local opportunities

The Volunteer Centre UK operates a service called Signposts which can
be used to find out about agencies in your area which have voluntary work
opportunities.

On receipt of your postcode and details of your interests Signposts can
supply you with a personalised printout listing current opportunities in
your area. They can also supply details of voluntary service bureaux
which may be able to help.

Details of the service and a volunteer form are available from:
Signposts, The Volunteer Centre UK, 29 Lower King's Road,
Berkhamsted, Hertfordshire HP4 2AB. Tel: (01442) 873311.

The Volunteer Centre also have a number of information sheets,
current price £1 each:

   13/502 'Volunteering Opportunities UK' (Opportunities for residential
   volunteers)
   13/504 'Volunteers' Welfare Benefits and Taxation'
   13/508 'Finding out about Volunteering in Your Area'
   13/512 'Volunteering and the Council Tax'
   13/513 'Volunteers Working with Children'
   13/523 'Volunteering Opportunities Overseas'.

France

About voluntary work in France

The voluntary work situation in France is broadly similar to that in the UK
with a wide range of voluntary agencies providing many types of service.
The voluntary sector is growing fast and many agencies have increased
their activities in recent years.

In addition to projects in France the French agencies also offer opportunities to work in other parts of the world, particularly French-speaking
countries in Africa, Asia and the Caribbean where they often outnumber
agencies from other parts of the world.

A knowledge of French is a major advantage. A limited number of
agencies can use non-French speakers.

Types of work available
France offers opportunities in most of the types of work covered in Chapter 2. Areas where voluntary agencies are expanding their operations are work with the young and the old, in conservation, and in disaster relief.

Sources to use
Write to voluntary agencies direct. If you speak some French, use the French state employment service, ANPE, and newspapers. Apart from the French newspapers there are some English-language newspapers in the south of France. It is also possible to call on voluntary agencies in person and ask, especially for summer jobs. Voluntary service bureaux include CIDJ (which can advise young people on summer jobs) and Cotravaux.

Visas and permits
UK nationals do not need a visa or a work permit in order to get a job in France. However, you will need a residence permit (called a Carte de Séjour) if you want to stay longer than three months. This can be obtained at the local town hall (known as the Mairie).

Other things you should know
Living costs in France are slightly less than in the UK, although accommodation is costly and hard to find in some places, especially the south and in Paris. Most employers pay higher wages than in the UK and there is a minimum national wage: 'le SMIC', although this does not apply to all voluntary work.

Useful contacts

Embassies
French Embassy, 58 Knightsbridge, London SW1X 7JT. Tel: (020) 7235 8030.
British Embassy, 35 rue de Faubourg St Honoré, 75008 Paris. Tel: 1 42 66 91 42.

Tourist Office in London
French Tourist Office, 178 Piccadilly, London W1V 0AL. Tel: (020) 7491 7622.

Main Tourist Offices
127 avenue des Champs Elysées, 75008 Paris. Tel: 1 42 23 61 72.
place Bellcour, Lyon. Tel: 478 42 25 75.
4 la Canebière, Marseille. Tel: 491 54 91 11.

State Employment Service
ANPE, 53 rue Général Leclerc, 92136 Issy les Moulineaux.

Private Employment Agencies
ECCO, 33 rue Raffet, 75016 Paris. Tel: 1 45 25 51 51.
Kelly, 50 avenue des Champs Elysées, 75008 Paris. Tel: 1 42 56 44 88.
Manpower, 9 rue Jacques Bingen, 75017 Paris. Tel: 1 47 66 03 03.

Newspapers
Le Monde, Le Figaro and *France-Soir* are the main national (Paris based) newspapers. The main regional newspapers are *Sud-Ouest* (Bordeaux), *La Voix du Nord* (Lille), *Ouest-France* (Rennes), *Le Progrès* (Lyon), *La Provençal* and *La Meridional* (Marseille). English language newspapers are *The News, Dordogne Telegraph* and *Riviera Reporter*.

Language Courses
Berlitz, 79 Wells Street, London W1A 3BZ. Tel: (020) 7637 0330.
Alliance Française, 6 Cromwell Place, London SW7 2JN. Tel: (020) 7723 6439.

Voluntary Service Bureaux
Association Montaigne, 83 boulevard de Montmorency, 75016 Paris.
CIDJ, 101 quai Branly, 75740 Paris.
Co-ordinating Committee for International Voluntary Service, 1 rue Miollis, 75015 Paris. Tel: 1 56 82 73 11.
Cotravaux, 11 rue de Clichy, 75009 Paris. Tel: 1 48 74 79 20.
Etudes et Chantiers Internationale, 33 rue Campagne Première, 75015 Paris.
Jeunesse et Reconstruction, 10 rue de Trevise, 75009 Paris.
The International Movement, 107 avenue du Général Leclerc, 95480 Pierrelaye.

Organisations running summer camps for children
ANSTJ, 17 avenue Gambetta, 91130 Ris-Orangis. Tel: 1 69 06 82 20.
CEMEA, 76 boulevard de la Villette, 75019 Paris. Tel: 1 42 06 38 10.
CPCV, 47 rue de Clichy, 75009 Paris. Tel: 1 42 80 06 99.
STAJ, 27 rue de ChÉteau d'eau, 75010 Paris. Tel: 1 42 08 56 63.
UCPA, 62 rue de la Glacière, 75640 Paris Cedex 13. Tel: 1 43 36 05 20.
UFVC, 19 rue Dareau, 75014 Paris. Tel: 1 45 35 25 26.

Voluntary Agencies
Action d'Urgence Internationale, 10 rue Felix Ziem, 75018 Paris. Tel: 1 42 64 75 88.

Afrique 2000, 16 rue des Ecoles, 75008 Paris. Tel: 1 43 29 86 20.

Aide et Action, 78 rue de la Réunion, 75020 Paris. Tel: 1 43 73 52 36.

Association de Paralysés de France, 17 boulevard Blanqui, 75013 Paris. Tel: 1 58 08 24 01.

Association des Trois Mondes (ATM), 63 bis rue du Cardinal Lenoine, 75005 Paris. Tel: 1 43 54 78 69.

Cue France, 107 rue de Longchamp, 75116 Paris. Tel: 1 47 04 27 11.

Croix Rouge Franáais, 1 place Henry Dunant, 75384 Paris. Tel: 1 45 68 27 31.

Enfants de Monde, 126 boulevard Vauban, 59800 Lille. Tel: 2 20 57 42 43.

Fondation de France, 40 avenue Hoche, 75008 Paris. Tel: 1 42 25 66 66.

Handicap Internationale, 18 rue de Gerland, 69007 Lyon. Tel: 4 78 61 17 37.

Inter Aide, 44 rue de la Paroisse, 78000 Versailles. Tel: 1 39 02 38 59.

International Medical Aid, 119 rue de Amanches, 75020 Paris. Tel: 1 46 36 04 04.

Médecins du Monde, 67 avenue de la République, 75541 Paris Cedex 11. Tel: 1 43 57 70 70.

Médecins Sans Frontières, 8 rue Saint Sabin, 75011 Paris. Tel: 1 40 21 29 29.

Ministère de la Culture, 4 rue d'Aboukir, 75002 Paris. Tel: 1 40 15 80 00.

Secours Catholique, 106 rue de Bac, 75340 Paris Cedex 07. Tel: 1 43 20 14 14.

Secours Populaire Français, 9 rue Froissant, 75003 Paris. Tel: 1 42 78 50 48.

Terre des Hommes France, 4 rue Franklin, 93200 Saint Denis. Tel: 1 48 09 09 76.

Spain

About voluntary work in Spain
Voluntary work opportunities in Spain are rather fewer than in other European countries. This is because of a greater reliance on self-help, but also because of increasing government provision; large amounts of money have been spent on public services.

The main thing to note is that great differences exist within Spain; Madrid, and the tourist areas such as the Costas, Balearic and Canary Isles are affluent, but many inland areas such as the Cantabrian Mountains and Sierra Morena suffer poverty and unemployment.

Types of work available
All types as discussed in Chapter 2. Most voluntary agencies work with

the young, with the old, or to relieve poverty. Many agencies are run by the Catholic Church. Few agencies work in conservation, or with animals. Many of the larger Spanish voluntary agencies have projects in South America.

Sources to use
Some vacancies are also advertised in *Overseas Jobs Express* and the national newspapers in the UK. Other than this it is quite difficult to locate vacancies from the UK. People with experience should register with the OPU. The Spanish national employment service, CNC, is rarely able to place foreigners. Newspapers are of some use and there are some English-language newspapers in the tourist areas.

A very common and well-accepted way of finding a job in Spain is either to write to prospective employers, or to visit them in person.

Visas and permits
UK nationals do not need a visa or a work permit in order to get a job in Spain. However, you will certainly need a residence permit (called a Residencia) if you want to stay longer than three months. This can be obtained at main police stations.

Other things you should know
Spain offers low living costs, especially out of the main resorts, although rates of pay are also lower than in the UK. Knowledge of Spanish is preferable as English is not spoken outside resorts.

Useful contacts

Embassies
Spanish Embassy, 24 Belgrave Square, London SW1X 8QA. Tel: (020) 7235 5555.
British Embassy, Calle de Fernando el Santo 16, Madrid 4. Tel: 91 319 0200.

Tourist Office in London
Spanish National Tourist Office, 57-58 James Street, London SW1. Tel: (020) 7499 0901.

Main Tourist Offices
Gran Via 658, Barcelona.
Torre de Madrid, Plaza Espana, Madrid. Tel: 91 241 2325.
Avenida Ray Jaime III 10, Palma de Mallorca.
Avenida de la Constitucion 21, Seville. Tel: 95 422 1404.

State Employment Service
INEM, General Pardinas 5, Madrid.

Private Employment Agencies
Restricted by law and can offer temporary jobs only.

Newspapers
El Pais, Diario 16 (Madrid), *El Diario de la Costa del Sol* (Malaga), *El Correo de Andalucia* (Seville). English-language newspapers include *Sur in English, Costa Blanca News, Iberian Daily Sun.*

Language Courses
Berlitz, 79 Wells Street, London W1A 3BZ. Tel: (020) 7637 0330.
Spanish Institute, 102 Eaton Square, London SW1. Tel: (020) 7235 1484.

Other Contacts
The Hispanic and Luzo Brazilian Council, 2 Belgrave Square, London SW1X 8PJ.

Voluntary Service Bureaux
Servicio Voluntario Internacional, Calle Ortega Y Gasset 71, Madrid 6.
TIVE, Calle Ortega Y Gasset 71, Madrid 6.
SCI-SCCT Catalunya, Rambla Catalunya, 08007 Barcelona.
Club de Relaciones Culturales Internacionales, Calle de Feraz 82, 28008 Madrid. Tel: 91 541 7103.

Voluntary Agencies
Action Aid, Caracas 21, Madrid 4. Tel: 91 400 0759.
Caritas Española, San Bernadino 99 bis 7, 28015 Madrid. Tel: 91 445 5300.
Cruz Roja Española, Eduardo Datio no. 16, 28010 Madrid. Tel: 91 419 7350.
Intermon, Roger de Lluria 15, 08010 Barcelona. Tel: 93 215 3723.
Medicos Sin Fronteras España, Lluis Sagnier 64-66, 08032 Barcelona. Tel: 93 347 1151.
Paz Y Cooperacion, Melendez Valdés 65, 28015 Madrid. Tel: 91 243 5282.
Solidaridad Internacional, Glorieta de Quevedo 7, 28015 Madrid. Tel: 91 593 1113.
SODEPAZ (Development and Peace), Calle Pizauro 5, 28004 Madrid. Tel: 91 552 8091.

Greece

About voluntary work in Greece
Greece is not at present a popular country for voluntary service. There is a strong tradition of self-help and community which solves many of the social problems that exist in other European countries.

Greece is an island nation whose cities, towns and villages are spread over thousands of islands large and small. This makes communications difficult, although travel services such as roads, air links and ferries are reasonably efficient considering the difficulties.

Types of work available
Although most types are available there is a predominance of two types. The first is community projects, particularly in remote, underdeveloped villages (some of which still have no road access). The second is in archaeology and conservation: Greece has thousands of important sites, many of which have yet to be investigated. Preserving and reinstating the national heritage is now taken very seriously.

Sources to use
It can be difficult to find work in Greece due to the word-of-mouth way in which work is traditionally found. Visiting the country is probably the best way to find a job. People looking to pre-arrange jobs should look in the *Overseas Jobs Express* newspaper. There are also some English-language newspapers in Athens which carry job vacancies. There are a growing number of private employment agencies in Greece. However, some of them may be unreliable in that the promised job is not available on arrival.

Visas and permits
UK nationals do not need a visa or a work permit in order to get a job in Greece. However, you will need a residence permit if you want to stay longer than three months. This can be obtained at the local police station or, in Athens, at the Ministry of Public Order.

Other things you should know
Greece has a very low cost of living, but wages are also much lower than in the UK. Many employers prefer to recruit staff on a casual/unofficial basis and may not always be reliable about paying wages.

Useful contacts

Embassies
Greek Embassy, 1A Holland Park, London W11 3TP. Tel: (020) 7727 8040.

British Embassy, 1 Ploutarchou Street, Athens 10675. Tel: 01 723 6211.

Tourist Office in London
4 Conduit Street, London W1R 0DJ. Tel: (020) 7734 5997.

Main Tourist Offices
Syntagma Square, Athens. Tel: 01 324 1884.

State Employment Service:
OAED, Thakris 8, 16610 Glyfada. Tel: 01 993 2589.

Private Employment Agencies
Athenian Agency, PO Box 511181. 14510 Kifissia, Athens. Tel: 01 808
    1005.
Camenos International Staff Consultancy, 12 Botsai Street, Athens
    147.
Intertom Agency, 24-26 Halkokondili Street, Athens 10432. Tel: 01 532
    9470.
Pioneer, 11 Nikis Street, Athens 10557. Tel: 01 332 4321.

Newspapers
The *Athens News* and *Athens Daily Post* are both English-language
newspapers.

Language Courses
Linguaphone, 124 Brompton Road, London SW3 2TL. Tel: 0800
    282417.

Voluntary Service Bureaux
STS, 1 Felellindy Street, Syntagma Square, Athens.
European Conservation Volunteers Greece, 15 Omirou Street, 14562
    Kifissia, Athens.
Service Civil International, 43 Avlonos Street, 10443 Athens.

Voluntary Agencies
Caritas Hellas, Caodistiou 52, 10432 Athens. Tel: 01 524 7879.
YWCA Greece, 11 Amerikas Street, 10672 Athens. Tel: 01 362 4294.
Hellenic Institute of Solidarity and Co-operation with Developing
    Countries, 9 Orminiou Street, 11528 Athens. Tel: 01 723 4456.
*Hellenic Red Cross, 1 Lycavittou Street, 10672 Athens. Tel: 01 362
    1681.*
Social Work Foundation, Mantzarou 6, 10672 Athens. Tel: 01 360
    7922.

Italy

About voluntary work in Italy
Italy has a large number of voluntary work opportunities. However, few foreign volunteers are attracted at present so it would be essential to speak some Italian to stand a reasonable chance of finding work here. Prospective volunteers should note the difference between the prosperous north of Italy, with rather less need for voluntary agencies, and the substantially poorer south.

Types of work available
People who speak good Italian may be able to find jobs in all the categories in Chapter 2. However, the main areas of voluntary work are in the relief of poverty, help for the aged, conservation, archaeology, and also medical charities. Many organisations are religiously-inspired and run by the Catholic Church.

Sources to use
Apply direct to voluntary agencies or voluntary service bureaux, either in the UK or Italy. Make use of church links as much as possible. People who speak some Italian should use the state employment agency, UCM. Newspapers are also a good source of vacancies for these people. There are no English-language newspapers. Personal visits may be successful if carefully planned.

Visas and permits
UK nationals do not need a visa or a work permit in order to get a job in Italy. However, you will need a residence permit (called a Carta di Soggiorno di Cittadino di Uno Stato Membro della CEE) if you wish to stay longer than three months. This can be obtained at the local police station (Questura, Commissariato or Stazione di Carabinieri).

Other things you should know
The cost of living and wages are quite high in northern Italy, but rather lower in the south.

Useful contacts

Embassies
Italian Embassy, 14 Three Kings Yard, London W1Y 2EH. Tel: (020) 7269 8200.
British Embassy, 80 Via Venti Settembre, 00100 Rome.

Tourist Office in London
1 Prince's Street, London W1R 8AY. Tel: (020) 7408 1254.
Main Tourist Offices
Via Parigi 5, Rome. Tel: 06 463748.
Piazza San Marco, Venice. Tel: 041 715555.
Via Cavour 1, Florence. Tel: 055 278785.

State Employment Service
Ufficio di Collocamento Mandopera, Via Pastrengo 16, Rome.

Private Employment Agencies
Not permitted in Italy.

Newspapers
Il Messaggero, Corriere della Sera, La Repubblica, La Voce Repubblicana (Rome), *La Nazione* (Florence), *Corriere della Serra, Il Giornale* (Milan), *La Stampa* (Turin), *Il Giornale di Napoli* (Naples), *Il Gazzetino* (Venice).

Language Courses
Berlitz, 79 Wells Street, London W1A 3BZ. Tel: (020) 7637 0330.
Inlingua, 8-10 Rotton Park Road, Birmingham B16 9JJ. Tel: (0121) 454 0204.

Voluntary Service Bureaux
Gruppi Archaeologici d'Italia, via Tacito 41, 00193 Rome. Tel: 06 687 4028.
Archeoclub d'Italia, Arco de 'Banchi 8, 00186 Rome.
Servizo Civile Internazionale, via de Laterani 28, 01184 Rome.
Movimento Christiano per la Pace, via Marco Dino Rossi 12C, 00173 Rome.
Associazione Italiana Construttori, via Cesare Battisti, 20071 Casalpusterlengo, Milan.

Voluntary Agencies
AMU (Action for a United World), Via Crescenzio 43, 00193 Rome. Tel: 06 654 4859.
ACAV, Via della Orfane, 38100 Trento. Tel: 0461 32319.
Association for International Development, Via Luigi Lillio 19, 60142 Rome. Tel: 06 592 3443.
Caritas Internationalis, Palazzo San Catisto, 00120 Vatican City. Tel: 06 698 7197.
Caritas Italiana, Viale F. Baldelli 41, 00199 Rome. Tel: 06 541 0281.

Centro Internazionale Crocevia, Via Merulana 247, 00185 Rome. Tel: 06 731 6841.

Controinformazione Terzo Monde (CTM), Via Nicola Calaldi 21, 73100 Lece. Tel: 0832 648736.

Croce Rossa Italiana, Via Toscana 12, 00187 Rome. Tel: 06 49991.

International Documentation and Communication Centre, Via S. Maria dell Anima 30, 00186 Rome. Tel: 06 686 8332.

ISIS, Via San Sabastian 5, 00153 Rome. Tel: 06 574 6479.

Servicio Volontario Internazionale (SUI), Via Tosio 2, 25121 Brescia. Tel: 030 295621.

Terra Nuova Centro per Il Volontario, Via Urbana 156, 00184 Rome. Tel: 06 474 7859.

Volontari Italiani Solidarieta Paesi Emergenti (VISPE), Via della Chiesa 3, 20084 Casirale Olonadi Lacchiarella, Milan. Tel: 02 524 2941.

Volontario Internazionale per Lo Sviluppo (VIS), Piazza Rebaudengo 22, 10155 Turin. Tel: 011 296967.

Portugal

About voluntary work in Portugal
Portugal is one of the least prosperous countries in Europe and has much need for voluntary assistance in some places. However, the family unit is strong. Organisation of many voluntary projects is poor. There are comparatively few voluntary agencies and, at present, very few foreigners doing this type of work.

The south and Lisbon are relatively prosperous; the inland areas of the Alentejo and Beira are substantially poorer.

Types of work available
The largest voluntary agencies work in relief of poverty, and with the elderly, young people and disabled. There are some medical charities. Many projects are operated by the Catholic Church. There are some conservation projects but relatively few as Portugal is not rich in archaeological sites.

Sources to use
Apply to UK agencies in the first instance. Also consider making a written, telephone or personal application to Portuguese agencies. Newspapers could be tried but offer limited potential. No employment agencies offer jobs of this type.

Visas and permits
UK nationals do not need a visa or a work permit in order to get a job in

Portugal. However, you will need a residence permit (called a Residància) if you want to stay longer than three months. This can be obtained at the local Serviáio de Estrangeiros (Alien Registration Office).

Other things you should know
Portugal offers a low cost of living together with lower wages than in the UK. It is not essential to speak Portuguese to get most jobs in voluntary work, but an advantage. As employment of EU citizens has only very recently been permitted, many employers are not yet used to employing non-Portuguese workers.

Useful contacts

Embassies
Portuguese Embassy, 11 Belgrave Square, London SW1X 8PP. Tel: (020) 7235 5331.
British Embassy, Rua de S. Domingos à Lapa, 1200 Lisbon. Tel: 01 396 1191.

Tourist Office in London
1-5 New Bond Street, London W1Y 0NP. Tel: (020) 7493 3873.

Main Tourist Offices
Praça do Restauradores, Lisbon. Tel: 01 571745.
Rua da Misericórdia, Faro, Algarve.
Largo Marquês de Pombal, Lagos, Algarve.

State Employment Service
Ministério de Trabalho, Praça de Londres, 1091 Lisbon Codex.

Private Employment Agencies
Do not usually offer voluntary work.

Newspapers
Correio de Manha, O Diario, Diario de Noticias, Jornal O Dia (Lisbon), *Jornal de Noticias* (Oporto). English-language newspapers include *Portugal Post, Algarve News, Anglo-Portuguese News* and *Madeira Island Bulletin*.

Language Courses
Linguaphone, 124 Brompton Road, London SW3 2TL. Tel: 0800 282417.
Portuguese Language School, PO Box 70, London SW15. Tel: (020) 8877 1738.

Other contacts
The Hispanic and Luzo Brazilian Council, 2 Belgrave Place, London
SW1X 8PJ.

Voluntary Service Bureaux
ATEJ (Associacao de Turismo Estudantil e Juvenil), PO Box 4586, 4009
Oporto.
Fundo de Apoio aos Organisms Juvenis (FAOJ), Rua Duque de Avila 137,
1097 Lisbon.
Companheiros Construtores, Rua Pedro Monteiro 3, 3000 Coimbra.
Instituto da Juventude, Avenida da Liberdade 194, 1200 Lisbon.
Ministério da Juventude, Estrada das Laranjeiras 197/205, 1600 Lisbon.
Tel: 01 726 5552.
Movimento Cristao Para a Paz (MCP), Rua António José Almeida 210.
3000 Coimbra.

Voluntary Agencies
Caritas Portuguesa, Estrado do Forte de Ameixoeira 19, 1700 Lisbon. Tel:
01 759 6046.
Centro de Informaçao e Documentaçao Amilar Cabral, Rua Pinheiro
Chaáas 77, 1000 Lisbon. Tel: 01 574718.
Coop Africa, Rua do Sacramento a Alcantara 38-1E, 1300 Lisbon. Tel: 01
437 3287.
Centro de Cultura e Estudos Rurais, Avenida Sidónio Pais 20, 1200
Lisbon. Tel: 01 549752.
OBRA, Rua da Ilha Principe 19, 1100 Lisbon. Tel: 01 814 8428.
OIKOS, Avenida Visconde Valmor, 35-3, 1000 Lisbon. Tel: 01 764719.

Germany

About voluntary work in Germany
As a very prosperous country Germany has less need for voluntary help
than other countries; however, work opportunities are good. German
voluntary agencies are usually very well funded and efficiently organised
and offer pay and conditions similar to the commercial business
sector.

Types of work available
There is no reason why those who speak fluent German should not be able
to compete for any of the jobs in Chapter 2. Most charitable projects
involve working with people – the old, young, disabled and refugees and
immigrants (mainly Turkish), many of whom have found it hard to adapt
to life in prosperous Germany.

Sources to use
The recruitment network in Germany is very well organised and all the methods discussed in Chapter 3 can be used. The state employment service, Arbeitsamt, is generally very helpful to foreigners and has a special bureau, called ZAV, which will deal with enquiries from the UK. However, private employment agencies are largely prohibited except for voluntary service bureaux. People who can speak German and offer a skill should register with the Overseas Placing Unit.

Most German national and regional newspapers carry a good selection of vacancies. However, few vacancies in Germany find their way into the UK press. Writing to employers in search of a vacancy can be successful in Germany.

Visas and permits
UK nationals do not need a visa or a work permit in order to get a job in Germany. However, you will need a residence permit (called a Aufenthaltserlaubnis) if you want to stay longer than three months. This can be obtained at the local town hall (known as the Rathaus).

Other things you should know
German wages are higher than in the UK, but German employers can be very demanding. Living costs are a little higher than in the UK. Although many Germans speak a little English, a knowledge of German is really essential.

Useful contacts

Embassies
German Embassy, 23 Belgrave Square, London SW1X 0PZ. Tel: (020) 7235 5033.
British Embassy, Friedrich-Ebert-Allee 77, 5300 Bonn. Tel: 0228 234061.

Tourist Office in London
61 Conduit Street, London W1R 0EN. Tel: (020) 7734 2600.

Main Tourist Offices
Europa Centre, Budapester Strasse, Berlin. Tel: 030 262 6031.
Hauptbahnhof, Frankfurt. Tel: 069230 5113.
Hauptbahnhof, Munich. Tel: 089 239 1256.
Klett Passage, Stuttgart. Tel: 0711 221453.

State Employment Service
Arbeitsamt, in most towns, but foreigners should contact ZAV,

Feuerbachstrasse 42, 6000 Frankfurt Am Main.

Private Employment Agencies
Mostly prohibited by law. However some temporary work bureaux, such as Manpower, and voluntary service bureaux, are permitted.

Newspapers
Frankfurter Allgemeine Zeitung, Die Welt (Frankfurt), *Süddeutsche Zeitung, Bayernkurier* (Munich), *Kölnsiche Rundschau* (Cologne), *Weser Kurier* (Bremen), *Stuttgarter Zeitung* (Stuttgart), *Berliner Morgenpost* (Berlin).

Language Courses
Berlitz, 79 Wells Street, London W1A 3BZ. Tel: (020) 7637 0330.
Goethe Institute, 50 Prince's Gate, London SW7 2PH. Tel: (020) 7581 3344.

Other Contacts
For jobs with children/summer camps:
TocH, National Projects Office, Forest Close, Wendover, Aylesbury, Buckinghamshire HP22 6BT. Tel: (01296) 623911.
British Forces Germany, BFG Youth Services, BFPO 140. Tel: 2161 472 3176.

Voluntary Service Bureaux
Aufbauwerk der Jugend Gemeinschaft für den Freiwilligen Internationalen Arbeitseinsatz, Bahnhofstrasse 26, 3350 Marburg.
Bund der Deutschen Katholischen Jugend (BDKJ) Jugendferienwerk, Antoniusstrasse 3, Postfach 1229, 7314 Wernau/N.
Deutscher Bundesjugendring, Haager Weg 44, 5300 Bonn 1.
Internationale Jugend-Gemeinschaftsdienste, Kaiserstrasse 43, 5300 Bonn 1.
Service Civil International Deutscher Zweig e.V., Blücherstrasse 14, 5300 Bonn 1.

Voluntary Agencies
Afrika-Verein, Neuer Jungfernstieg 21, 2000 Hamburg. Tel: 040 345051.
Brot für die Welt, Stafllenbergstrasse 76, Postfach 101142, 7000 Stuttgart. Tel: 0711 21590.
Bund der Deutschen Katholischen, Carl Mosterts Platz 1, 4000 Dusseldorf 30.
CVJM (YMCA Germany), Im Druseltal 8, Postfach 410149, 3500 Kassel Wilhelmshöhe.

Deutscher Entwicklungdienst (German Volunteer Service), Kladower
   Damn 299, Postfach 220035, 1000 Berlin 22. Tel: 030 365090.
Deutsche Sportjugend, Oto Fleck Schneise 12, 6000 Frankfurt 71.
German Red Cross, Friedrich Ebert Allee 71, Postfach 1460, 5300 Bonn
   1. Tel: 0228 5411.
Informationszentrum Dritte Welt, Kronenstrasse 1611, Postfach 53287,
   7800 Freiburg. Tel: 0761 74003.
Kindernothilfe (Children in Need), Düsseldorfer Landstrasse 180,
   Postfach 281143, 4100 Duisburg. Tel: 0203 77890.
Naturfreundejugend   Deutschlands   (Friends   of   Nature),
   Grossglocknerstrasse 28, 7000 Stuttgart 60.
Zentralstelle für Entwicklungshilfe (Catholic Aid), Mozartstrasse 9,
   Postfach 1450, 5100 Aachen. Tel: 0241 4429.

Belgium

About voluntary work in Belgium
Belgium has a large voluntary sector, which operates in most areas.
However, the situation varies across the country. Although generally a
very prosperous country, Belgium has social and economic problems in
some local areas, especially in the east, around Ieper, and the west, around
Diest.

Belgium is French speaking in the south and Flemish (Dutch) speaking in the north. Some knowledge of these languages is preferred,
although English is widely spoken in and around Brussels.

Types of work available
Most of the types of work as discussed in Chapter 2 are available. The
largest agencies work in medicine, with children, the old, poor and disabled, and with animals. A number of Belgian agencies work overseas,
particularly in Africa.

Sources to use
All the methods of finding work as discussed in Chapter 3 can be used in
Belgium. The state employment agency (called VDAB, FOREM or
ONEM depending on the area) will help foreigners. Special T-Service
bureaux offer temporary work. People with a language and skills to offer
should register with the OPU. There are also private agencies and volun-
tary service bureaux. Newspapers can be used for finding vacancies.
Brussels has an excellent English-language newspaper called *The
Bulletin*.

Visas and permits
UK nationals do not need a visa or a work permit in order to get a job in Belgium. However, you will need a residence permit if you want to stay longer than three months. This can be obtained at the local town hall.

Other things you should know
Belgium has the highest standard of living in Europe. Living costs and wages are slightly more than in the UK.

Useful contacts

Embassies
Belgian Embassy, 103 Eaton Square, London SW1X 9AB. Tel: (020) 7235 5422.
British Embassy, Britannia House, rue Joseph II 28, 1040 Brussels. Tel: 02 217 90 00.

Main Tourist Office
Hotel de Ville, Grand Place, 1000 Brussels. Tel: 02 513 8940.

State Employment Service
For Flanders: VDAB
For Wallonia: FOREM
Head office at boulevard de l'Empereur 7, 1000 Brussels.
In Brussels: ONEM, 38 rue d'Escalier, 1000 Brussels.
T-Service Bureau: 69 boulevard Anspach.

Private Employment Agencies
ECCO, 17a rue Vilian XIV, 1050 Brussels. Tel: 02 647 87 80.
Avenue Louise Interim, 207 avenue Louise, 1050 Brussels. Tel: 02 640 91 91.
Select Interim, 1-5 avenue de la Joyeuse Entrée, 1040 Brussels. Tel: 02 231 03 33.
Creyf's, 473 avenue Louise, 1050 Brussels. Tel: 02 646 34 34.

Newspapers
Le Soir (Brussels), *Antwerpse Morgan* (Antwerp), *La Meusse* (Liege). In Brussels also see *Belgique No. 1* (free), *L'Echo* (free) and *The Bulletin* (English language).

Language Courses
Berlitz, 70 Wells Street, London W1A 3BZ. Tel: (020) 7637 0330.
Inlingua, 8-10 Rotton Park Road, Birmingham B16 9JJ. Tel: (0121) 454 0204.

Voluntary Service Bureaux

Annee Diaconale Belge, Service Protestant de la Jeunesse, Rue de
    Champs de Mars 5, 1050 Brussels, Belgium. Tel: 02 513 2401.

Archeolo-J, Avenue Paul Terlinden 23, 1330 Rixenstart. Tel: 02 653 8268.

Bouworde VZW, Tiensesteenweg 145, 3010 Kessel Lo.

Carrefour Chantiers, 25 boulevard de l'Empereur, 1000 Brussels.

Entraide et Amitie ASBL, 9 rue du Boulet, 1000 Brussels. Tel: 02 512 3632.

Service Civil International, rue Van Elewyck 35, 1050 Brussels.

Vrijwillige Internationale Aktie, Draakstraat 37, 2018 Antwerp.

Voluntary Agencies

Association Europe Tiers Monde (ETM), Rue de la Loi 200, 1049
    Brussels. Tel: 02 235 8634.

Association Internationale des Charities, Rue d'Alsace Lorraine 38, 1050
    Brussels. Tel: 02 512 3898.

ATD Quart Monde, Avenue Victor Jacobs 12, 1040 Brussels. Tel: 02 647
    9900.

Centre National de Cooperation Au Développement, Quai du Commerce
    9, 1000 Brussels. Tel: 02 218 4727.

Croix Rouge de Belgique, Chaussée de Vleurgat 88, 1050 Brussels. Tel:
    02 647 1010.

Euro Caritas Association Internationale, Rue du Commerce 72, 1040
    Brussels. Tel: 02 511 4255.

Foster Parents Plan Belgie, F. Laurentplein 11, 9000 Ghent. Tel: 091
    242373.

Handicap International, Rue du Toulouse, 1040 Brussels. Tel: 02 230 1050.

Les Amis des Iles de Paix et de l'Action, Rue du Marché 37, 5200 Huy.
    Tel: 085 230454.

Jeunesse Ouvrière Chrétienne Internationale (JOCI), Rue Plantin 11, 1070
    Brussels. Tel: 02 521 6983.

Les Magasins du Monde – Oxfam, Rue de la Caserne 74, 1000 Brussels.
    Tel: 02 511 8709.

Médecins Sans Frontières Belgique, 24-26 Rue Deschampheleer, 1080
    Brussels. Tel: 02 310605.

Oxfam Belgique, Rue du Conseil 39, 1050 Brussels. Tel: 02 512 1487.

Youth Forum of the European Communities, Rue de la Science 10, 1040
    Brussels. Tel: 02 230 6490.

The Netherlands

About voluntary work in the Netherlands

The Netherlands has a large and well-developed voluntary sector. The
situation is very similar to that in the UK in that both state provision and

charitable activity work alongside each other in many cases of need. There are many voluntary agencies here and most of them are well funded and very well organised.

English is spoken by many people, but a knowledge of Dutch is an advantage.

Types of work available
Most of the types of work discussed in Chapter 2 are available in the Netherlands. In particular, a large number of charities work with young people, offering education, advice, activities and social guidance. Most of the larger Dutch agencies also work extensively in disaster relief and relief of poverty in other countries of the world.

Sources to use
The job-finding network in the Netherlands is very well developed and an agency is usually the best way of finding work. People with a knowledge of Dutch should register with the OPU. The Netherlands employment service will help foreigners to find work, but it is better to call on them in person. The Netherlands also has a very large network of private employment agencies, known as Uitzendbureaux, which can almost always offer some type of short-term work. Also use the voluntary service bureaux.

Newspapers usually carry a large number of vacancies. However, there are no suitable English-language newspapers. Vacancies are rarely advertised in the UK.

Approaching employers direct is also to be recommended and can be done in person, by post, or by 'phone, as many employers speak at least a little English.

Visas and permits
UK nationals do not need a visa or a work permit in order to get a job in the Netherlands. However, you will need a residence permit if you want to stay longer than three months. This can be obtained from a main police station.

Other things you should know
Living costs are very similar to the UK; perhaps a little more for some purchases. Wages are higher than in the UK and a legal minimum wage exists for all employees over 23.

Useful contacts

Embassies
Royal Netherlands Embassy, 38 Hyde Park Gate, London SW7 5DP. Tel: (020) 7584 5040.

British Embassy, Lange Voorhout, The Hague 2514 ED. Tel: 070 364 5800.

Tourist Office in London
25 Buckingham Gate, London SW1E 6LD. Tel: (020) 7630 0451.

Main Tourist Offices
Centraal Station, Amsterdam. Tel: 020 626 6444.
Den Hague CS, The Hague. Tel: 070 354 3501.
State Employment Service
Singel 202, 1016 AA Amsterdam. Tel: 020 520 0911.
Begynenhof 8, 5611 EL Eindhoven. Tel: 040 325325.
Engelse Kamp 4, 9722 AX Groningen. Tel: 050 225911.
Troelstrakade 65, 2531 AA The Hague.
Schiedamse Vest 160, 3011 BH Rotterdam.

Private Employment Agencies
Manpower, Van Baerlestraat 16, Amsterdam. Tel: 020 664 4180.

Newspapers
De Telegraaf, De Volkskrant, Het Parool (Amsterdam), *Haagsche Courant* (The Hague), *Utrechts Nieuwsblad* (Utrecht).

Language Courses
Linguaphone, 124 Brompton Road, London SW3 2TL. Tel: 0800 282417.

Other Contacts
Central Bureau Arbeidsvoorziening, Postbus 415, 2280 AK Rijswijk. Tel: 070 313 0911. (Can find and advise on temporary work for young people; all types of industry.)

Voluntary Service Bureaux
Dutch Volunteers Liaison Committee, Keizergraant 181, 1016 DR Amsterdam. Tel: 020 257212.
ICVD, Pesthuislaan 25, 1054 RH Amsterdam.
SIW Internationale Vrijwilligers Projekten, Willemstraat 7, 3511 RJ Utrecht. Tel: 030 317721.
Vrijwillige Internationale Aktie, Pesthuislaan 25, 1054 RH Amsterdam.

Voluntary Agencies
Afrika Centrum, Rijksweg 15, 6267 AC Maastricht. Tel: 043 071226.
Arlsen Zonde Grenzen Nederland (Médecins Sans Frontières),

Reguliersbreestraat 12, Postbus 10014, 1001 EA Amsterdam. Tel: 020 251272.

Third World Information Centre, Simon Stevinweg 17, Postbus 750, 5201 AT s'Hertogenbosch. Tel: 073 218970.

Caritas Netherlands, Hekekkaan 6, Postbus 1041, 5200 DA Den Bosch. Tel: 073 144544.

Centrum Kontakt der Kontinenten, Amersfoortsestraat 20, 3769 AS Soesterberg. Tel: 034 631755.

Service Abroad, Zusterplein 22A, Postbus 177, 3700 AD Zeist. Tel: 03404 24884.

Interserve, Krakelingweg 10a, 3707 HV Zeist. Tel: 03404 13741.

Leger des Heils (Salvation Army), 15 Damstraat, 1012 JL Amsterdam. Tel: 020 241703.

SAWA, Schoolplein 7, 3581 DX Utrecht. Tel: 030 340958.

Stichting Kinderhulpplan, Nassaulaan 15, 2264 Leidschendam. Tel: 070 327 6790.

Dutch Interchurch Help, Cornelis Houtmanstraat 17, Postbus 13077, 3507 LB Utrecht.

Save the Children Netherlands, Postbus 30470, 2500 GL Den Haag. Tel: 070 652250.

Tear Fund Netherlands, Hoofdstraat 55, Postbus 104, 3970 AC Driebergen-Rijsenburg. Tel: 034 381 4844.

YWCA Nederland, F.C. Donderstraat 23, 3572 JB Utrecht. Tel: 030 715525.

Ireland

About voluntary work in Ireland
The voluntary work situation in Ireland is very similar to that in the UK. Indeed, many Irish charities mirror the work of their colleagues in the UK and employ people with similar skills. The main difference is that a large number of charitable organisations are religiously motivated.

Types of work available
The fact that English is spoken in Ireland means that most of the jobs as discussed in Chapter 2 are available to applicants from the UK. The main areas of voluntary work available are work in hospitals, and with the elderly, the disabled and children. There are also many reform and pressure groups and educational organisations.

Sources to use
All the methods of finding a job, as discussed in Chapter 3, may be used. Vacancies are advertised in UK as well as Irish newspapers. The state

employment agency FÁS can be tried. Writing letters to prospective employers can also be successful although personal application is also worth considering.

The Institute of Public Administration (IPA) Administration Yearbook and Diary lists many voluntary agencies and government contacts in Ireland. This is available at many reference libraries in the UK.

Visas and permits
UK citizens do not need a visa, work permit or residence permit to live and work in Eire. However, you do need to take a full passport.

Other things you should know
The costs of living in Ireland is similar to or higher than in the UK, although rates of pay are no higher. Income taxes are generally higher.

Useful contacts

Embassies

Irish Embassy, 17 Grosvenor Place, London SW1X 7HR. Tel: (020) 7235 2171.
British Embassy, 33 Merrion Road, Dublin 2. Tel: 01 764088.

Tourist Office in London
Ireland House, 150 Bond Street, London W1. Tel: (020) 7493 3201.

Main Tourist Offices
Grand Parade, Cork. Tel: 021 543289.
14 Upper O'Connell Street, Dublin. Tel: 01 747733.

State Employment Service
FÁS, 65a Adelaide Road, Dublin 2. Tel: 01 765861.

Private Employment Agencies
A list is available from FAS.

Newspapers
The Irish Independent (see Thursday), *The Irish Times* (see Friday), *The Irish Press.*

Voluntary Service Bureaux
An Oige, 39 Mountjoy Square, Dublin 1. Tel: 01 363111.
Comhchairdeas, 7 Lower Ormond Quay, Dublin 1. Tel: 01 729681.

The Community and Youth Information Centre, Sackville House, Sackville Place, Dublin 1. Tel: 01 786844.

Groundwork Ireland, 43 Bayview Drive, Killiney, Co Dublin. Tel: 01 822563.

Voluntary Service International, 37 North Great George's Street, Dublin 1. Tel: 01 788679.

Voluntary Agencies

An Taisce (Irish National Trust), Tailor's Hall, Back Lane, Dublin 8. Tel: 01 541786.

Christian Aid, Rathga Road, Dublin 6. Tel: 01 966184.

Concern, 1 Upper Camden Street, Dublin 2. Tel: 01 754162.

Goal, PO Box 19, Dunlaoghaire, Co Dublin. Tel: 01 809779.

Irish Red Cross Society, 16 Merrion Square, PO Box 1312, Dublin 2. Tel: 01 765135.

Irish Wildlife Conservation, Ruttledge House, 8 Longford Place, Monkstown, Co. Dublin.

Oxfam in Ireland, 202 Lower Rathines Road, Dublin. Tel: 01 972195.

Simon Community, PO Box 1022, Lower Sheriff Street, Dublin 1. Tel: 01 711606.

VMM, High Park, Grace Park Road, Dublin 9. Tel: 01 376565.

World Vision in Ireland, 38 Upper Baggot Street, Dublin 4. Tel: 01 609432.

Scandinavia: Denmark, Finland, Norway, Sweden

About voluntary work in Scandinavia
The potential for voluntary workers in Scandinavia is more limited than elsewhere. These countries have high taxes and so a very high standard of government provision as regards public services.

Types of work available
All types of work discussed in Chapter 2 are available, but to a very limited extent. Chiefly, these involve giving some extra help to the disadvantaged old, young and disabled. There are also many animal and conservation charities. Many Scandinavian voluntary agencies direct their help to third world charities, working to relieve poverty or cope with natural disasters.

Sources to use
The main sources to use are the state employment agencies, newspapers, and direct application to employers. There are many private employment agencies in Denmark but few elsewhere.

Visas and permits
In Norway a work permit may be needed before leaving the UK, although this requirement is being phased out under the EEA (European Economic Area) agreement between the EU and Norway. Check the current situation with the Embassy.

Other things you should know
All the Scandinavian countries are substantially more expensive to live in than the UK; accommodation is particularly expensive. Rates of income tax are high.

Useful contacts

Denmark
Danish Embassy, 55 Sloane Street, London SW1X 9SR. Tel: (020) 7333 0200.
British Embassy, Kastelvej 38-40, 2100 Copenhagen. Tel: 33 246600.
Danish Tourist Office, Sceptre House, 169-173 Regent Street, London SW1X 9SR. Tel: (020) 7235 1255.

Main Tourist Offices
8 Østerå, Aalborg.
22 H.C. Andersen Boulevard, Copenhagen. Tel: 33 111325.
Skolegade 33, Esbjerg. Tel: 75 124258.

State Employment Agency
Arbejdsformidlingen, Adelgade 13, Copenhagen 1304.

Newspapers
Politiken, Ekstra Bladet, Den Bla Auis, Belingske Tidende, Det Fri Aktuelt, Fryerns Stiftstidente, Vestkystem.

Voluntary Service Bureaux and Voluntary Agencies
ASF- Dansk Folkenjaelp, Roskilderej 147, PO Box 206, 2620 Albertslund. Tel: 52 64 06 00.
Cooperative Centre Denmark, Vesterbrogade 4A3, 1503 Copenhagen V. Tel: 33 32 38 11.
Dansk Røde Kois (Danish Red Cross), Dag Hammarskjölds Alle 28, PO Box 2600, 2100 Copenhagen 0. Tel: 01 38 14 44.
Danish UN Association, Kronprinsensgade 9, 1114 Copenhagen K. Tel: 01 12 39 39.

Danchurchaid, Sankt Peders Straede 3, 1453 Copenhagen K. Tel: 11 15 28 00.
International Youth Exchange, Borgergade 14, 1300 Copenhagen K.
Mellemfolkelight Samvirke, Borgerade 10-14, Copenhagen K. (Danish Centre for International Cooperation).
Swallows of Denmark, Osterbrogade 86, 2100 Copenhagen. Tel: 11 26 17 47.

Finland
Finnish Embassy, 38 Chesham Place, London SW1X 8HW. Tel: (020) 7235 9531.
British Embassy, Itainen Puistotie 17, 00140 Helsinki. Tel: 90 661293.
Finnish Tourist Office, 66 Haymarket, London SW1Y 4RF. Tel: (020) 7839 4048.

Main Tourist Offices
Pohjoiseplanadi 19, Helsinki. Tel: 90 1693757.
Hatanpään, Tampere.
Käsityöläiskatu 3, Turku.

State Employment Agency
Ministry of Labour, PO Box 524, Eteläesplanadi 4, 00100 Helsinki 10.

Newspapers
Turun Sanomat, Aamulehti, Helsingin Sanomat.

Voluntary Service Bureaux and Voluntary Agencies
Finnish Family Programme, PO Box 343, 00531 Helsinki.
Finn Solidarity, PO Box 146, 00531 Helsinki. Tel: 90 7011 817.
Finnish Volunteer Service, Freduikinkatu 63, 00100 Helsinki. Tel: 90 69 41004.
Finnchurchaid, Luotsikatu 1, PO Box 185, 00161 Helsinki. Tel: 90 18021.
Finnish Red Cross, Tehtaankatu 1a, PO Box 168, 00141 Helsinki. Tel: 90 12931.
International Solidarity Work, Kotkankatu 11, 00150 Helsinki. Tel: 90 77081.
International Voluntary Workcamps Finland, Rauhanasema Veturitori, 00520 Helsinki.
Service Civil International, Rauhanasema Veturitori, 00520 Helsinki 52.

Norway
Norwegian Embassy, 39 Eccleston Street, London SW1W 9NT. Tel: (020) 7730 9900.

British Embassy, Thomas Heftyesgate 8, 0244 Oslo 2. Tel: 02 55 24 99.
Norwegian Tourist Office, 5 Lower Regent Street, London W1. Tel: (020)
    7839 6255.

Main Tourist Offices
Torgallmenning, Bergen. Tel: 05 31 32 75.
Radhusplassen, Oslo. Tel: 02 83 00 50.
Torvet, Trondheim. Tel: 07 53 04 90.

State Employment Agency
Arbeidsdirektoratet, Postboks 8127 Dep, Oslo 00332. Tel: 01 11 10 70.

Newspapers
Dagbladet, Aftenposten, Arbeiderbladet.

Voluntary Service Bureaux and Voluntary Agencies
APØG, Lokkegt 23, 2600 Lillehammer.
Atlantis – The Norwegian Council for Youth Exchange, Rolfhofmosgate
    18, Oslo 6. Tel: 02 670043.
Care Norge, PO Box 8226, Hammersborg, 0129 Oslo 1. Tel: 02
    425218.
Caritas Norge, Fagerbogt 17, 0360 Oslo 3. Tel: 02 693015.
Nansen Centre, Barnegarden Breivold, Nesset, 1400 Ski.
Norwegian Church Aid, Underhaugveien 15, PO Box 5868, 0308 Oslo 3.
    Tel: 02 463970.
Norges Blindeforbund (Aid to the Blind), Sporveisgaten 10, PO Box
    5990, Hegdehaugen. 0308 Oslo 3. Tel: 02 466990.
Norges Døveforbuno (Aid for the Deaf), Sven Bruns Gaten 7, PO Box
    6850, 0130 Oslo 1. Tel: 01 111775.
Norges Handikapforbund, Nilsltamsensvei 2, PO Box 49, 0611 Oslo 6.
    Tel: 02 648610.
Quaker Service Norway, Meltzers Gaten 1, 0257 Oslo 1. Tel: 02 440178.
Service Civil International, Langesgate 6, 0165 Oslo 1.

Sweden
Swedish Embassy, 11 Montagu Place, London W1H 2AL. Tel: (020) 7724
    2101.
British Embassy, Skarpögatan, 11527 Stockholm. Tel: 08 667 0149.
Swedish Tourist Office, 3 Cork Street, London W1X 1HA. Tel: (020)
    7437 5816.

Main Tourist Offices
Kungsportsplatsen, Gothenburg.

Färjeleden 3, Visby, Gotland. Tel: 0489 16933.
Västra Boulevarden, Kristianstad.
Norrmalm, Stockholm. Tel: 08 789 2000.

State Employment Agency
Arbetmarknadsstryrelsen, Box 634, Vasagatan 28-34, 510130
Stockholm.

Newspapers
*Svenska Dagbladet, Dagen, Expressen, Dagnes Nyheter, Gîteborg
Posten.*

Voluntary Service Bureaux and Voluntary Agencies
Bålsla Jordvänner (Friends of the Earth), Norra Villavägen 7, 19800
   Bålsla. Tel: 0171 56296.
Church of Sweden Aid, Box 297, 751015 Uppsala. Tel: 018 169500.
Diakonia, Älvsjö Gårdsväg 3, 12530 Alvsjö. Tel: 08 749 1500.
Frälsningsarmen (Salvation Army), Östermalmsgatan 71, Box 5090,
   10242 Stockholm. Tel: 08 663 1700.
Service Civil International, Barnangsgatan 23, 11641 Stockholm.
Swallows in Sweden, Spolegatan 5, 22220 Lund. Tel: 046 121005.
U-Assist, 16187 Stockholm. Tel: 08 797 1606.
Volunteer Organisations Information Centre, Hornsgatan 54, 11721
   Stockholm. Tel: 08 449185.
YMCA, Box 2054, 10212 Stockholm. Tel: 08 145330.
YWCA, Box 2054, 10212 Stockholm. Tel: 08 145330.

REST OF EUROPE

Switzerland

About voluntary work in Switzerland
As a prosperous country Switzerland has minimal need for voluntary
agencies, but these do exist and offer some potential for the foreign worker. The main point to note about this type of work in Switzerland is that a
large number of agencies work mainly to aid those in other countries
worldwide, rather than in Switzerland itself.

Types of work available
The International Red Cross was established in Switzerland in 1864 and
Switzerland is home to many international disaster relief organisations
and also to campaign and pressure groups. There is also work with the dis-

advantaged, especially the young, old, poor and drug users etc. Conservation of the lakes and mountains is a growing activity; the Swiss are very green-minded.

Sources to use
The best way of finding work is to apply direct to the organisations which operate in Switzerland. A few vacancies are advertised in the UK press and in *Overseas Jobs Express*.

Foreigners cannot generally use the Swiss national employment service and few private employment agencies deal with these jobs. Local newspapers are of some limited use.

Visas and permits
Swiss employers are allocated a number of combined visa and work/residence permits which they can give out to foreign workers of their choice, rather than the employee having to apply for the permit as happens elsewhere. However, the numbers are limited and so finding work depends on finding an employer with permits available. This also applies to most voluntary workers.

As Switzerland has agreed with the European Union countries (of which Switzerland is not a member) to relax these controls, these permits may be abolished in the future. You are advised to check the current situation with the Embassy.

Other things you should know
Switzerland is an extremely expensive country in which to live. Accommodation can be very expensive and hard to find. Wages are high by UK standards.

Switzerland has three official languages (French, German and Italian) depending on the area, or canton, in which you are working. Knowledge of one of these is an advantage.

Useful contacts

Embassies
Swiss Embassy, 16-18 Montagu Place, London W1H 2BQ. Tel: (020) 7723 0701.
British Embassy, Thunstrasse 50, 3000 Berne. Tel: 031 445021.

Tourist Office in London
Swiss Centre, 1 New Coventry Street, London W1V 3HG. Tel: (020) 7734 1921.

Main Tourist Offices
Gare Cornavin, Geneva. Tel: 022 731 6450.
Bahnhofplatz 15, Zurich. Tel: 01 482 3544.
Schifflande 15, Basle.
Bahnhof, Berne.

Newspapers
Neue Zurcher Zeitung (Zurich), *Basler Zeitung, Baslerstab* (Basle),
Berner Zeitung, Berner Tagwacht (Berne), *La Suisse, La Tribune de
Genève, Journal de Genève* (Geneva).

Language Courses
The official languages of Switzerland are French, German and Italian. See
relevant country sections for details of language courses.

Other Contacts
Summer camps for children:
Village Camps, Chalet Seneca, 1854 Leysin. Tel: 041 25 34 23 38.

Voluntary Service Bureaux
Gruppo Voluntari Della Svizzera Italiana, PO Box 12, 6517 Arbedo.
IBG – Internationale Begegnung in Gemeinschaftsdiensten Ev,
    Sclosserstrasse 28, 7000 Stuttgart 1.
Service Civil International, Postfach 228, 3000 Bern 9.

Voluntary Agencies
ATD Quart Monde, 1733 Treyvaux.
Bellerne Found, 4 Rue Munier Rommilly, 1211 Geneva 3. Tel: 022
    468866.
Centrale Sanitaire Suisse, CP 145, 8031 Zurich.
Helvetas, St Moritzstrasse 15, 8042 Zurich. Tel: 01 363 5060.
Interaid, Schaffhauserstrasse 210, 8052 Zurich.
International Save the Children Alliance, 147 Rue de Lausanne, 1202
    Geneva. Tel: 022 217016.
League of Red Cross and Red Crescent Societies, 17 Chemin des Crets,
    CP 372, 1211 Geneva 19. Tel: 022 345580.
Médecins Sans Frontières Suisse, 10 Chemin de Malombe, 1206 Geneva.
    Tel: 022 471500.
Swissaid, Jubilämsstrasse 60, CP34, 3006 Bern. Tel: 031 449555.
YWCA, 37 quai Wilson, 1201 Geneva. Tel: 022 323100.
World Vision International, Chemin de la Tourelle, 1209 Geneva. Tel: 022
    798 4183.

Austria

About voluntary work in Austria
As a prosperous country Austria does not have a great deal of demand for voluntary services, but they still operate both within the country and outside, especially in providing help to eastern Europe.

Types of work available
Main opportunities are in work with the disadvantaged – old, young, poor, drug users etc. Agencies working outside the country are involved with refugee aid programmes.

Sources to use
The only effective way of pre-arranging work is to apply to the agencies of your choice in both the UK and Austria. A small number of vacancies are advertised in the *Overseas Jobs Express*. Casual jobs can sometimes be found by visiting Austria. Newspapers are of limited use. The state employment agency (Landesarbeitsamt) can help foreign workers.

Visas and permits
EU nationals do not need a work permit in order to work legally in Austria. A residence permit is needed for stays over three months.

Other things you should know
The cost of living and wages offered in Austria are significantly higher than in the UK, although not as high as in Switzerland. A knowledge of Austrian German is desirable; this is quite different from the German spoken in Germany.

Useful contacts

Embassies
Austrian Embassy, 18 Belgrave Mews West, London SW1X 8HU. Tel: (020) 7235 3731.
British Embassy, Jauresgasse 12, A-1010 Vienna. Tel: 01 713 1575.

Main Tourist Office
Herrengasse 16, Graz. Tel: 0316 914076.
Kärntnerstrasse 38, Vienna. Tel: 0222 586 3246.

State Employment Services
Bebenbergerstrasse 33, A-8021 Graz.
Schöpfstrasse 5, Innsbruck.

Schiesstantstrasse 4, A-5021 Salzburg.
Hohenstauffengasse 2, A-1013 Vienna. (Region)
Weihburggasse 30, Vienna. (City)

Private Employment Agencies
Do not normally deal with work of this type.

Newspapers
Die Press, Der Standard, Wiener Zeitung (Vienna), *Neue Tiroler Zeitung,
Tiroler Tageszeitung, Salzburger Volkszeitung* (Salzburg).

Language Courses
Berlitz, 79 Wells Street, London W1Z 3BZ. Tel: (020) 7637 0330.
Further information available from the Anglo-Austrian Society, 46 Queen
    Anne's Gate, London SW1H 9AU. Tel: (020) 7222 0366.

Other Contacts
Summer camps for children:
Young Austria, Alpenstrasse 108a, 5020 Salzburg.

Voluntary Service Bureaux
ÖKISTA, Garnisongasse 7, 1090 Vienna.
Österreichischer Bauorden. PO Box 186 Hornegasse 3, 1031 Vienna.
Service Civil International, Schottengasse 3a, 1010 Vienna.

Voluntary Agencies
Action 365, Bäckerstrasse 18, 1010 Vienna. Tel: 0222 527960.
Development Aid, Böcklinstrasse 44, Postfach 250, 1020 Vienna. Tel:
    0222 532561.
Hilfe für Alle (Help for All), Staudinggergasse 11, 1200 Vienna. Tel: 0222
    331425.
Menschen für Menschen (People for People), Capistrangasse 8-10, 1060
    Vienna. Tel: 0222 563206.
Caritas Austria, Nibelungengasse 1, Postfach 114, 1011 Vienna. Tel: 0222
    587 1577.
Rettet Das Kind (Save the Children), Pouthongasse 3, 1150 Vienna. Tel:
    0222 926216.
Österreichischer Informationsdienst für Entwicklungspolitik, Tuchlauben
    8-16, 1010 Vienna. Tel: 0222 533 3755.
Hilfe für Kinder in Not (Children in Need), Züglergasse 49, 1070 Vienna.
    Tel: 0222 963120.
World Vision International, Mariahilferstrasse 10, 1070 Vienna. Tel: 0222
    961333.

Turkey

About voluntary work in Turkey
Turkey is a relatively new country for the voluntary worker, but undoubt-
edly much is to be done – especially in the inland areas away from the
tourist resorts. As well as its own national voluntary agencies Turkey
receives help from western European agencies and a number of UK agencies currently have projects there.

At present, voluntary work in Turkey is not well organised. Most
opportunities are for unpaid work or on short contracts rather than regular full-time jobs.

Types of work available
Many voluntary agencies work in social provision. This includes working
in hospitals, and with children, the elderly and the poor. Most western
agencies work mainly in eastern Turkey, helping to relieve the impact of
natural disasters, although these areas also have political difficulties and
so are to be avoided by the inexperienced.

Turkey is also home to many historic and archaeological sites and the
majority of foreign workers are involved in excavation and restoration.

Sources to use
The only effective method of pre-arranging a job is to write to UK
charities which work in Turkey. Otherwise use the voluntary service
bureaux in the UK and Turkey. Few other methods are likely to succeed;
no employment agencies can help foreigners and newspapers are also of
little use, although there is an English-language newspaper in Istanbul.

Visas and permits
As Turkey is not a member of the European Union all UK citizens who
want to work there must obtain a working visa. This is applied for by your
employer once you have found a job.

Other things you should know
Turkey has a very low cost of living. Wages are also much lower than the
UK and employers are not always reliable about making payment. It is not
necessary to speak any Turkish to find work.

Useful contacts

Embassies
Turkish Embassy, 43 Belgrave Square, London SW1X 8PA. Tel: (020)
7235 5222.

British Embassy, Sehit Ersan Caddesi 46a, Ankara. Tel: 04 127 4310.

Tourist Office in London
170-173 Piccadilly, London W1V 9DD. Tel: (020) 7734 8681.

Main Tourist Offices
Divanyolu Caddesi, Istanbul. Tel: 01 522 4903.
Iskele Meydani, Bodrum.

Newspapers
Daily News (English language).

Language Courses
Berlitz, 79 Wells Street, London W1A 3BZ. Tel: (020) 7637 0330.
Inlingua, 8-10 Rotton Park Road, Birmingham B16 9JJ. Tel: (0121) 454 0204.

Voluntary Service Bureaux
Genctur Turizm ve Seyahet Acentasi Ltd, 15/3 Yerebatan Caddesi, 34410
    Sultanahmet, Istanbul. Tel: 01 526 5409.
Concordia Youth Service Volunteers Ltd., 8 Brunswick Place, Hove,
    Sussex BN3 1ET. Tel: (01273) 772086.
GSM Youth Activities Service, Yüksel Caddesi 44/6, 06420 Kizilay,
    Ankara. Tel: 041 332200.
International Voluntary Service (IVS), Old Hall, East Bergholt,
    Colchester CO7 6TQ. Tel: (01206) 298215.
Silatur, 11 Emek Ishani Kat, Kizilay, Ankara. Tel: 041 181326.
UNICEF Türkiye Millikomitesi, Abdullah Cevdet Sokak, 20/10
    Camkaya, Ankara. Tel: 041 138 1745.
United Nations Association (Wales), International Youth Service, Temple
    of Peace, Cathays Park, Cardiff CF1 3AP. Tel: (029) 2022 3088.

Eastern Europe

About voluntary work in Eastern Europe
Eastern Europe is one of the newest areas in which voluntary agencies
operate and many, both from the individual eastern European countries
and other countries worldwide, are now working here. The situation
varies considerably, with some countries requiring extensive support from
voluntary agencies but others very little.

Most foreigners working in these areas are with UK and western
European-based agencies. The number of openings available with eastern
European organisations is quite limited.

Types of work available
All types of work are available, but these are mainly in areas of social need – relief of poverty and working with the young, old and disabled. Some projects are involved in education and conservation. Whilst the disaster relief organisations are providing 'first aid' help in eastern Europe, many agencies are involved in promoting self-help and long-term development.

Sources to use
In the first place, people seeking work should contact UK voluntary agencies working in eastern Europe. Secondly, try the voluntary service bureaux in the relevant country. It is very difficult to deal with voluntary agencies in each country direct. Some jobs are advertised in national newspapers in the UK, and also in *Overseas Jobs Express*.

People possessing useful skills, experience and qualifications may consider contacting the London Embassies of each country. Eastern European governments sometimes recruit specialists, or know of voluntary aid programmes that are in operation or forthcoming.

Visas and permits
Work permits and visas are needed for all these countries. These will be arranged by employers once you have found a job. In some cases voluntary workers are exempt.

Other things you should know
Rates of pay in eastern Europe are extremely low, although those working for UK agencies will often receive UK rates of pay. In most places facilities, such as travel and accommodation, are still way behind the rest of Europe.

Useful contacts

Voluntary Agencies Working in Eastern Europe
BEARR Trust (British Emergency Action in Russia and the Republics), 40 Holborn Viaduct, London EC1P 1AJ. Tel: (020) 7353 3090.
British Executive Service Overseas (BESO), 164 Vauxhall Bridge Road, London SW1V 2RB. Tel: (020) 7630 0644.
British Red Cross Society, 9 Grosvenor Crescent, London SW1X 7EJ. Tel: (020) 7235 5454.
Christian Children's Fund of Great Britain, 52 Bedford Row, London WC1R 4LR. Tel: (020) 7831 7145.
East Anglian Appeal for Romania, 5 Faversham Road, Beckenham, Kent BR3 3PN. Tel: (020) 8658 9207.

East European Partnership, Carlton House, 27A Carlton Drive, London SW15 2BZ. Tel: (020) 8780 2841.

Hamlet Trust, 9 Clifton Road, London W9 1SZ. Tel: (020) 7289 1587.

International Voluntary Service (IVS), Old Hall, East Bergholt, Colchester CO7 6TQ. Tel: (01206) 298215.

Operation Romanian Villages, 54 Waldemar Avenue, London SW6 5NA. Tel: (020) 7731 4133.

Salvation Army, 101 Queen Victoria Street, London EC4P 4EP. Tel: (020) 7236 5222.

Bulgaria

Bulgarian Embassy, 186 Queen's Gate, London SW7 5HL. Tel: (020) 7584 9400.

British Embassy, Boulevard Marshal Tolbukin 65-67, Sofia. Tel: 02 879575.

Bulgarian Tourist Office, 18 Prince's Street, London W1R 7HE. Tel: (020) 7499 6988.

Voluntary Service Bureau
Argo-M, Boulevard Stambolski 2A, Sofia 1000.

Czech Republic

Czech Embassy, 25 Kensington Palace Gardens, London W8 4QY. Tel: (020) 7727 3966.

British Embassy, Mala Strana, Thunovska Ulice 14, 12550 Prague 1. Tel: 02 533347.

Czech Tourist Office, 17-18 Old Bond Street, London W1X 8RB. Tel: (020) 7629 6058.

Voluntary Service Bureaux
Brontosaurus, Kancelar Brontosaura, Bubenska 6, 17000 Prague 7. Tel: 02 802910.

INEX, Gorkehonam 24, 116547 Prague 1.

KMC – Klub Maldychcestovatelu, Male Strana 1, 11800 Prague 1.

Estonia

Estonian Embassy, 16 Hyde Park Gate, London SW7 5DG. Tel: (020) 7589 3428.

Hungary

Hungarian Embassy, 35 Eaton Place, London SW1X 8BY. Tel: (020) 7235 2664.

British Embassy, Harmincad Utca 6, Budapest V. Tel: 1 118 2888.
Hungarian Tourist Office, 6 Conduit Street, London W1R 9TG. Tel: (020)
   7493 0263.

State Employment Service
Katona J. Utca 25, Budapest. Tel: 1 122 294.
Bokány D. Utca 2a, Budapest. Tel: 1 124 630.
Széchenyi Tér 9, Pécs. Tel: 72 13 721.
Bajcsy Zs. Utca 4, Szeged. Tel: 62 22 890.
Csaba Utca 26, Györ. Tel: 96 11 180.

Voluntary Service Bureau
Unio Youth Workcamps Association, Kun. B 37-38, 1138 Budapest.

Latvia
Latvian Embassy, 72 Queensborough Terrace, London W2 3SP. Tel: (020)
   7727 1698.

Lithuania
Lithuanian Embassy, 17 Essex Villas, London W8 7BP. Tel: (020) 7937
   1588.
British Embassy, Hotel Riga, Aspazijasbul 2, 226050 Riga. Tel: 0132
   226050.

Voluntary Service Bureaux
International Exchange Centre, 2 Republic Square, 226168 Riga, Latvia.
Centre of Student Activities, K Donelacio 73-113 3006 Kaunas,
   Lithuania.

Poland
Polish Embassy, 47 Portland Place, London W1N 3AG. Tel: (020) 7580
   5481.
British Embassy, 1 Aleja Róz, 00556 Warsaw. Tel: 02 228 1001.
Polish Tourist Office, 82 Mortimer Street, London W1N 7DE. Tel: (020)
   7580 8028.

Voluntary Service Bureaux
Almatur, 9 Ordynacka Street, 00953 Warsaw. Tel: 26 23 56.
OHP, Nowy Swiat 18-20, 00920 Warsaw. Tel: 32 43 99.
Polish Foundation for International Youth Exchanges, Ul. Grzybowska
   79, 00844 Warsaw.

Romania

Romanian Embassy, 4 Palace Green, London W8 4QD. Tel: (020) 7937 9666.

British Embassy, 24 Strada Jules Michelet, 70153 Bucharest.

Romanian Tourist Office, 17 Nottingham Place, London W1M 3FF. Tel: (020) 7224 3692.

Russia

Russian Embassy, 13 Kensington Palace Gardens, London W8 4QX. Tel: (020) 7229 3628.

British Embassy, Naberezhnaya Morisa Toreza 14, Moscow 72.

Voluntary Service Bureaux

Sputnik, 15 Kosygin Street, Moscow 117946.

Youth Voluntary Service, 7 Bol Komsomolski, Moscow 103982.

Ukraine

British Embassy, Room 1008, Zhoutneva Hotel, Ulitsa Rozi Luxembourg, 252021 Kiev. Tel: 044 291 8907.

Voluntary Service Bureaux

UFIYC, Lvov Polytechnic Institute, 12 Mira St, 290646 Lvov.

5
Guide to Voluntary Work:
Rest of the World

NORTH AMERICA

About voluntary work in the USA and Canada
The USA and Canada have very large voluntary sectors. Despite being a wealthy country, the USA in particular has great contrasts between rich and poor, and voluntary agencies are called in to help in many areas where there is no government provision. In addition to domestic voluntary agencies both the USA and Canada have a large number of agencies which work abroad, particularly in the poor countries of South America. Voluntary agencies in both countries are well organised and funded and in the USA are often operated like commercial businesses.

The main problem for people seeking work is that both countries impose strict visa requirements and this makes it extremely difficult for foreigners to work in, for example, Miami or Vancouver. Unless you can find an employer willing to employ you, with no one else locally able to do that work (which is very unlikely), then your chances of obtaining a visa are quite remote.

No UK voluntary agencies work in these countries.

Types of work available
All types of work are available, as discussed in Chapter 2, However, the main areas are international disaster relief, international aid, education and development and work with the poor – young, old, disabled and minority groups. Reform and pressure groups are also very active.

Sources to use
For jobs in these countries it is advisable to apply direct by letter or 'phone to voluntary agencies. A very small number of vacancies are advertised in the UK national newspapers and *Overseas Jobs Express*.

Visas and permits
You must have a working visa to take up a job in the USA or Canada. This

can only be applied for, to the appropriate Embassy, once you have found a job and before travelling to the country concerned. Most voluntary workers enter on the exchange programme J-1 visa (USA).

Other things you should know
Although many opportunities for voluntary work are available in these countries, it is very difficult to get a visa for permanent migration and/or full-time paid work. Instead consider unpaid voluntary work to provide experience of work in these countries.

Useful contacts

Canada
Canadian High Commission, Trafalgar Square, London SW1Y 5BJ. Tel: (020) 7629 9492.
British High Commission, Elgin Street, Ottawa K1P 5K7. Tel: 0613 237 1530.
Canadian Tourist Programme, Trafalgar Square, London SW1Y 5BJ. Tel: (020) 7629 9492.

Provincial information offices
Alberta: 1 Mount Street, London W1Y 5AA.
British Colombia: 1 Regent Street, London SW1Y 4NS.
Nova Scotia: 14 Pall Mall, London SW1Y 5LU.
Quebec: 59 Pall Mall, London SW1Y 5HJ.
Ontario: 21 Knightsbridge, London SW1Y 7LY.
Saskatchewan: 16 Berkeley Street, London W1X 5AE.

Voluntary Service Bureaux and Voluntary Agencies
Canadian Baptist Overseas Mission, 7185 Millcreek Drive, Mississauga, Ontario L5N 5R4. Tel: 416 821 3533.
Canadian Bureau for International Education, 14th Floor, 85 Albert Street, Ottawa, Ontario K1P 6A4.
Canadian Council of Churches, 40 St Clair Avenue E, Toronto, M4T 1M9. Tel: 416 921 4152.
Co-Development Canada, 1672 10th Avenue, Vancouver V5N 1X5. Tel: 604 873 5011.
Canadian Foundation for World Development, 2441 Bayview Avenue, Willowdale, Ontario M2L 1A5. Tel: 416 445 4740.
Canadian National Parks Service, 25 Edyy Street, Ottawa, Ontario K1A 0H3. Tel: 819 994 5127.
Disabled People International, 504 Donald Street, Winnipeg, Manitoba R3B 2H8. Tel: 204 942 3604.

Friends of the Earth, 251 Laurier Avenue West, Ottawa K1P 5J6. Tel: 613 230 3352.

Frontiers Foundation, Suite 203, 2615 Danforth Avenue, Toronto, Ontario M4C 1L6. Tel: 416 690 3930.

Oxfam Canada, 251 Laurier Avenue West, Ottawa K1P 5J6. Tel: 613 237 5236.

The Salvation Army, PO Box 4021, Toronto M5W 2B1. Tel: 416 598 2071.

World Vision Canada, 6630 Turner Valley Road, Mississauga, Ontario L5N 2S4. Tel: 416 821 3030.

USA

United States Embassy, 24 Grosvenor Square, London W1V 2JB. Tel: (020) 7499 9000.

Visa Branch, 5 Upper Grosvenor Square, London W1A 2JB. Tel: (020) 7499 3443.

British Embassy, 3100 Massachusetts Avenue NW, Washington DC 20009. Tel: 202 462 1340.

Tourist office contacts in USA
Alaska: Tel: 907 465 2020.
California: Tel: 916 322 1396.
Florida: Tel: 904 487 1462.
Hawaii: Tel: 808 923 1811.
Massachusetts: Tel: 617 727 3201.
Mississippi: Tel: 1 800 647 2290.
New York: Tel: 518 474 4116.
Texas: Tel: 512 475 5956.
Washington DC: Tel: 202 789 7000.

Voluntary Service Bureaux and Voluntary Agencies
America's Development Foundation, 600 South Lee Street, Alexandria VA22314. Tel: 703 836 2717.

American Jewish World Service (AJWS), 729 Boylston Street, Boston MA02116. Tel: 617 267 6656.

American Red Cross, 17th and D Street NW, Washington DC20006. Tel: 202 737 8300.

Assistance International, PO Box 955, Long Beach CA90802. Tel: 213 432 3016.

CARE, 660 First Avenue, New York NY10016. Tel: 212 686 3110.

Catholic Relief Services (CRS), 1011 First Avenue, New York NY10022. Tel: 212 838 4700.

Church World Service, 475 Riverside Drive, New York NY10115-0500. Tel: 212 870 2061.

Concern America, 2024 W Broadway, Suite 205, PO Box 1790, Santa Anna CA92706. Tel: 914 953 8575.

Friends of the Third World, 611 West Wayne Street, Fort Wayne IN46802. Tel: 219 422 6821.

Intermedia, 475 Riverside Drive, Room 670, New York NY10115. Tel: 212 870 2376.

Christian Aid, 5189 Verdugo Way, Camarillo CA93010. Tel: 805 987 8888.

International Executive Service Corps, PO Box 10005, Stanford, Connecticut. Tel: 203 967 6000.

International Human Assistance Programs, 360 Park Avenue South, New York NY10010. Tel: 212 684 6804.

Mercy Corps International (MCI), 3030 SW First Avenue, Portland OR97201. Tel: 503 223 0501.

National Cooperative Business Association, 1401 New York Avenue NW, Suite 1100, Washington DC20005. Tel: 202 638 6222.

Operation Crossroads Africa, 150 Fifth Avenue, Suite 310, New York NY10011. Tel: 212 242 8550.

Opportunity International, PO Box 3695, Oak Brook IL60522. Tel: 312 279 9300.

Overseas Development Council (ODC), 1717 Massachusetts Avenue NW, Suite 501, Washington DC20036. Tel: 202 234 8701.

Overseas Development Network, PO Box 2303, Stanford CA94309. Tel: 415 725 2869.

Oxfam America, 115 Broadway, Boston MA02116. Tel: 617 482 1211.

Pan American Development Foundation, 1889 F Street NW, Washington DC20006. Tel: 202 458 3972.

Private Agencies Collaborating Together, 777 UN Plaza, New York NY10017. Tel: 212 692 9748.

Rehabilitation International, 1133 Avenue of the Americas, New York NY10036. Tel: 212 869 8500.

The Rotary Foundation, 1600 Ridge Avenue, Evanston IL60201, Tel: 312 328 0100.

Salvation Army, 1025 Vermont Avenue NW, Suite 305, Washington DC2005. Tel: 202 737 3330.

Save the Children, 54 Willon Road, Westport CT06880. Tel: 202 226 7271.

Technoserve, 148 East Avenue, Norwalk CT06851. Tel: 203 582 0377.

Tolstoy Foundation, 200 Park Avenue South, New York NY10003-1522. Tel: 212 677 7770.

Volunteers International, 10701 Main Street, Fairfax VA22030. Tel: 703 352 7550.

World Concern, PO Box 33000, Seattle WA98133. Tel: 206 546 7201.

World Vision International, 919 West Huntingdon Drive, Monrovia
CA91016. Tel: 818 303 8811.
YMCA of the USA, 101 North Wacker Drive, Chicago IL60606. Tel: 312
977 0031.
YWCA of the USA, 726 Broadway, New York NY10003. Tel: 212 614
2700.
Jobs in summer camps and working with children
BUNAC, 16 Bowling Green Lane, London EC1R 0BD. Tel: (020) 7251
3472.
CampAmerica, 37a Queens Gate, London SW7 5HR.

CENTRAL AND SOUTH AMERICA

About voluntary work in these countries
Central and South America have some of the greatest need for voluntary
services in the world. Many of these countries suffer from political problems and severe poverty, and are prone to natural disasters. There is very
little government help for their communities.

Programmes are operated by local voluntary agencies, as well as those
from the USA and western Europe. Local agencies tend to lack organisation, and this is typical of the area as a whole where even well-organised
international agencies find it difficult to get things done.

Types of work available
All types, but principally working with the elderly, young, disabled, poor
and minorities, especially on care, educational and medical programmes.
Many voluntary agencies are religiously motivated. Conservation is a
growing area of activity.

Sources to use
The only effective way to locate a vacancy is to apply direct to UK voluntary agencies which operate in South America. Also consider voluntary
agencies in the USA. People with some language knowledge will find that
some European agencies (particularly in Spain) also work in South
America. Foreign Embassies sometimes know of forthcoming programmes and may pass on advice. Any visit to South America should be
very carefully planned in advance.

Visas and permits
A working visa is required for all these countries and should be applied
for from the London Embassy of the relevant country once you have
found a job.

Other things you should know
Wages and living costs in this part of the world are much lower than in the UK. In many places travel and other facilities are very basic. The standard of living can be very low and some countries have political and public order problems.

Useful contacts

UK Voluntary Agencies Working in South America
BAM (Freres des Hommes UK), 8 St Michael's Road, London SW9 0SL.
CAFOD, Romero Close, Stockwell Road, London SW9 9TY. Tel: (020) 7733 7900.
Catholic Institute for International Relations, 3 Canonbury Yard, New North Road, London N1 7BJ. Tel: (020) 7354 0883.
Christian Children's Fund of Great Britain, 52 Bedford Row, London WC1R 4LR. Tel: (020) 7831 7145.
Environmental Network for Nicaragua, 129 Seven Sisters Road, London N7 7QC. Tel: (020) 7272 9619.
Health Unlimited, 3 Stamford Street, London SE1 9NT. Tel: (020) 7928 8105.
Help the Aged, St James's Walk, London EC1R 0BE. Tel: (020) 7253 0253.
Nicaragua Health Fund, 83 Margaret Street, London W1N 7HB. Tel: (020) 7580 4292.
Oxfam, 274 Banbury Road, Oxford OX2 7DZ. Tel: (01865) 311311.
Peace Brigades International, 5 Caledonian Road, London N1 9DX. Tel: (020) 7713 0392.
St Andrews Evangelical Mission, 126 Ealing Road, Brentford, Middlesex TW8 0LD.
St Joseph's Hospice Association, La Casa de San Jose, Ince Road, Liverpool L23 4UE.
War on Want, 37 Great Guildford Street, London SE1 0ES. Tel: (020) 7620 1111.

USA Voluntary Agencies Working in South America
The American Friends Service Committee, 1501 Cherry Street, Philadelphia PA19102.
Amigos de las Americas, 5618 Star Lane, Houston TX 77057.
Los Niños, 1330 Continental Street, San Ysidro CA92073.
National Central America Health Rights Network, 853 Broadway, Suite 416, New York NY10003.
Nature Conservancy Association, 1800 North Kent Street, Suite 800, Arlington VA22209.
Nicaragua Network, Suite 212, 2025 I Street NW, Washington DC20006.

The Overseas Development Network, PO Box 1430, Cambridge MA02238.

Ventana, 339 Lafayette Street, New York NY10012.

Winant Clayton Volunteer Association, 43 Trinity Square, London EC3N 4DJ.

Other Contacts

The Hispanic and Luzo Brazilian Council, 2 Belgrave Square, London SW1X 8PJ.

Argentina

Argentine Embassy, 53 Hans Place, London SW1X 0LA. Tel: (020) 7584 6494.

British Embassy, Dr Luis Agote 2412, 1425 Buenos Aires.

Brazil

Brazilian Embassy, 32 Green Street, London W1Y 4AT. Tel: (020) 7499 0877.

British Embassy, Setoe de Embaixadus Sul, Quadra 801, Conjunto K, 70.408 Brazilia DF. Tel: 061 225 2710.

Brazilian Tourist Office, 35 Dover Street, London W1. Tel: (020) 7499 0877.

British and Commonwealth Chamber of Commerce, Caixa Postal 669ZC00, Sao Paulo.

Colombia

Colombian Embassy, 3 Hans Crescent, London SW1X 0LR. Tel: (020) 7589 9177.

British Embassy, Torre Propaganda Sancho, Calle 98 No. 9-03 Piso 4, Bogota. Tel: 01 218 5111.

Chile

Chilean Embassy, 12 Devonshire Street, London W1N 2DS. Tel: (020) 7580 6392.

British Embassy, Avenida El Bosque Norte 0125, Casilla 72-D, Santiago. Tel: 02 231 9771.

Voluntary Service Bureau

Cadesur, Calle Serrano 347, Casilla 109, Castro.

Costa Rica

Costa Rican Embassy, 14 Lancaster Gate, London W2 3LH. Tel: (020) 7723 1772.

British Embassy, Apartado 815, Centro Colon 1007, San José. Tel: 215566.

Voluntary Service Bureaux
ICADS, 2070 Sabanilla, San José 250508.
OTEC, Avenida 3, Calle 3-5, San José.

Cuba
Cuban Embassy, 167 High Holborn, London WC1V 6PA. Tel: (020) 7240 2488.
British Embassy, Edificio Bolívar, Cárcel 101-103, E Morro Y Prado, Apartado 1069, Havana. Tel: 07 623071.

Voluntary Service Bureau
Cuba Solidarity Campaign, Priory House, Kingsgate Place, London NW6. Tel: (020) 7388 1429.

Mexico
Mexican Embassy, 8 Halkin Street, London SW1X 7DW. Tel: (020) 7235 6393.
British Embassy, Calle Rio Lerma 71, Colonia Cuauhtémoc, 06500 Mexico City DF. Tel: 05 207 20 89.
Mexican Tourist Office, 7 Cork Street, London W1X 1PB. Tel: (020) 7434 1058.

Voluntary Service Bureaux
AMISTOUR, Versalles 35-502, 06600 Mexico City DF.
Vimex, Alfredo Elizando 69, CP 15450, Mexico City DF.
SETEJ, Hamburgo 301, Col. Juarez, 06600 Mexico City DF.

Nicaragua
Nicaraguan Embassy, 8 Gloucester Road, London SW7 4PP.
British Embassy, PO Box A169, El Reperto Los Robles, Primera Etapa, Entrada Principal de la Carretera Masaya, Managua. Tel: 02 70034.

Venezuela
Venezuelan Embassy, 1 Cromwell Road, London SW7 2HW. Tel: (020) 7584 4206.
British Embassy, Apartado 1246, Caracas 1010A. Tel: 02 751 1022.
Venezuelan Tourist Office, 1 Cromwell Road, London SW7 2HW. Tel: (020) 7584 4206.

AFRICA

About voluntary work in these countries
The African countries are more in need of voluntary help than any other part of the world. Almost every country has severe problems of one type or another, and receives support from many other foreign countries in addition to the services provided by its own organisations.

The most important point to note about working in Africa is that most jobs are for those with skills, experience and qualifications. Africa has no shortage of unskilled labour, so if you want to work here you should have something extra to offer an employer.

Types of work available
The main type of work is disaster relief, although often this work is carried out on a permanent basis. Many agencies are involved working with the poor, old and young, and particularly refugees. Not all the work involves providing stop-gap aid, however. Educational and intermediate technology agencies also operate extensively with the aim of trying to avoid future disasters.

Sources to use
Jobs in Africa are most usually found by applying direct to voluntary agencies in the UK. Some jobs are also advertised in the UK national newspapers. Foreign embassies will also sometimes advise. It is also possible to apply direct by letter to African voluntary agencies, although communications difficulties should be expected.

Visas and permits
A working visa is required for all these countries and should be applied for to the London embassy of the relevant country once you have found a job. Voluntary agencies will usually help you with the procedure.

Other things you should know
English is widely spoken in many African countries, particularly the Commonwealth nations. A knowledge of French, or an African language, is often an advantage. Most jobs are on fixed-term contracts. Accommodation is usually provided but working conditions can be difficult and dangerous in some cases.

Useful contacts

UK Voluntary Service Bureaux and Voluntary Agencies
Action Water, Mount Hawke, Truro TR4 8BZ. Tel: (01209) 715385.

Africa Inland Mission International, 2 Vorley Road, London N19 5HE. Tel: (020) 7281 1184.

Africa Now, Bovis House, Townmead Road, London SW6 2RH. Tel: (020) 7371 5603.

BAM (Freres des Hommes UK), 8 St Michael's Road, London SW9 0SL.

British Red Cross Society, 9 Grosvenor Crescent, London SW1X 7EJ. Tel: (020) 7235 5454.

CAFOD, Romero Close, Stockwell Road, London SW6 9TY. Tel: (020) 7733 7900.

Catholic Institute for International Relations, 3 Canonbury Yard, New North Road, London N1 7BJ. Tel: (020) 7354 0883.

Christian Aid, Interchurch House, 35 Lower Marsh, London SE1 7RL. Tel: (020) 7620 4444.

Evergreen Trust, 50 Wilton Street, Old Basford, Nottingham NG6 0ER. Tel: (0115) 9791404.

Friends of Africa International Christian Ministry, 13 Glebe Road, Brampton, Cambridgeshire PE1 8PH. Tel: (01480) 450989.

Help the Aged, St James's Walk, London EC1R 0BE. Tel: (020) 7253 0253.

Intermediate Technology Development Group, Myson House, Railway Terrace, Rugby CV21 3HT. Tel: (01788) 560631.

Oxfam, 274 Banbury Road, Oxford OX2 7DZ. Tel: (01865) 311311.

Save the Children Fund, 17 Grove Lane, London SE5 8RD. Tel: (020) 7703 5400.

Skillshare Africa, 3 Belvoir Street, Leicester LE1 6SL. Tel: (0116) 254 0517.

Voluntary Service Overseas, 317 Putney Bridge Road, London SW15 2PN. Tel: (020) 8780 2266.

War on Want, 37-39 Great Guildford Street, London SE1 0ES. Tel: (020) 7620 1111.

WaterAid, 1 Queen Anne's Gate, London SW1H 9BT. Tel: (020) 7233 4800.

World Vision of Britain, Dynchurch House, 8 Abington Street, Northampton NN1 2AJ. Tel: (01604) 22964.

African Voluntary Service Bureaux and Voluntary Agencies

African-American Institute, 833 UN Plaza, New York NY10017, USA.

Africa Voluntary Service, Private Bag 717, Freetown, Sierra Leone.

Alliance des Unions Chrétiennes de Jeunes Gens du Cameroon, BP13183 Doula, Cameroon.

Association Culturelle des Activités d'Amité et d'Echanges, Centre Culturel, Niacira, Algeria.

Association Tunisienne d'Action Volontaire, Boulevard 9 Avril 1938, 1002 Tunis, Tunisia.

Chantiers Sociaux Marocains, PO Box 456, Rabat, Morocco.

Christian Council of Kenya, Ufungamano House, Mamlaka Road, PO Box 54579, Nairobi, Kenya.

Jeunesse et Cooperation, PO Box 19, Safi, Morocco.

Kenyan Voluntary Development Association, PO Box 48902, Nairobi, Kenya.

Lesotho Workcamps Association, PO Box MS6, Maseru 100, Lesotho.

Nigerian Voluntary Service Association, PO Box 11837, Ibadan, Nigeria.

Pensée et Chantiers, PO Box 1423, Rabat, Morocco.

Voluntary Association of Ghana, PO Box 1540, Accra, Ghana.

Algeria

Algerian Embassy, 54 Holland Park, London W11 3RS. Tel: (020) 7221 7800.

British Embassy, 7 Chemin Capitaine Slimane Hocine, El Mouradia, Algiers. Tel: 02 606601.

Egypt

Egyptian Embassy, 26 South Street, London W1Y 6EL. Tel: (020) 7499 2401.

British Embassy, Ahmed Ragheb Street, Garden City, Cairo. Tel: 02 354 0850.

Egyptian Tourist Office, 168 Piccadilly, London W1Y 9DE. Tel: (020) 7493 5282.

Ethiopia

Ethiopian Embassy, 17 Prince's Gate, London SW7 1PZ. Tel: (020) 7589 7212.

British Embassy, Fikre Mariam Abatechan Street, PO Box 858, Addis Ababa. Tel: 01 612354.

Gambia

Gambia High Commission, 57 Kensington Court, London W8 5DG. Tel: (020) 7937 6316.

British High Commission, PO Box 507, 48 Atlantic Road, Banjul. Tel: 95133.

Ghana

Ghana High Commission, 104 Highgate Hill, London N14 0BZ. Tel: (020) 8342 8686.

British High Commission, PO Box 296, Osu Link, Accra. Tel: 021 221665.

Kenya

Kenyan High Commission, 45 Portland Place, London W1N 4AS. Tel: (020) 7636 2371.

British High Commission, PO Box 30133, Bruce House, Standard Street, Nairobi. Tel: 02 335944.

Kenyan Tourist Office, 13 New Burlington Street, London W1X 1FF. Tel: (020) 7839 4477.

Morocco

Moroccan Embassy, 49 Queen's Gate, London SW7 5NE. Tel: (020) 7581 5001.

British Embassy, 17 Boulevard de la Tour Hassan, BP45, Rabat. Tel: 720905.

Moroccan Tourist Office, 174 Regent Street, London W1R 6HB. Tel: (020) 7437 0073.

Mozambique

Mozambique Embassy, 21 Fitzroy Square, London W1P 5HJ. Tel: (020) 7383 3800.

British Embassy, Avenida I Lenine 310, CP55, Maputo. Tel: 01 420111.

Nigeria

Nigerian High Commission, Nigeria House, 9 Northumberland Avenue, London WC2N 5BX. Tel: (020) 7839 1244.

British High Commission, 11 Eleke Crescent, Lagos. Tel: 01 619531.

Somalia

Somali Embassy, 60 Portland Place, London W1N 3DG. Tel: (020) 7580 7148.

South Africa

South African Embassy, Trafalgar Square, London WC2N 5DP. Tel: (020) 7839 2211.

British Embassy, 6 Hill Street, Arcadia, Pretoria 0002. Tel: 012 433121.

South African Tourist Office, 1-4 Warwick Street, London W1R 5WB. Tel: (020) 7439 9661.

Sudan

Sudan Embassy, 3 Cleveland Row, London SW1A 1DD. Tel: (020) 7839 8080.

British Embassy, PO Box 801, Khartoum. Tel: 011 70760.

Tanzania
Tanzanian High Commission, 43 Hertford Street, London W1Y 8DB. Tel: (020) 7499 8951.
British High Commission, Hifadhi House, Samora Avenue, PO Box 9200, Dar Es Salaam. Tel: 051 29601.

Tunisia
Tunisian Embassy, 29 Prince's Gate, London SW7 1QC. Tel: (020) 7584 8117.
British Embassy, BP229, 5 Place de la Victoire, Tunis 1015RP. Tel: 01 245100.
Tunisian Tourist Office, 7a Stafford Street, London W1. Tel: (020) 7499 7679.

Zambia
Zambian High Commission, 2 Palace Gate, London W8 5NG. Tel: (020) 7589 6655.
British High Commission, PO Box 50050, Independence Avenue, Lusaka. Tel: 01 228955.
Zambian Tourist Office, 163 Piccadilly, London W1V 9DE. Tel: (020) 7498 1188.

Zimbabwe
Zimbabwe High Commission, 429 Strand, London WC2R 0SA. Tel: (020) 7836 7755.
British High Commission, PO Box 4490, Stanley House, Jason Moyo Avenue (PO Box 4490), Harare. Tel: 04 793781.
Zimbabwe Tourist Office, 52-53 Piccadilly, London W1V 9AA. Tel: (020) 7629 3955.

ASIA

About voluntary work in these countries
The situation as to voluntary work opportunities in Asia is mixed. In this continent there are both very wealthy and very poor countries. The countries of the Middle East, for example, have little need for voluntary help. There are a few opportunities in Israel, Syria and Jordan. The countries of the Far East also offer a mixed prospect. Some countries have need of voluntary service, particularly those in Indo-China; others are more wealthy and self-reliant than is often expected. India and other countries of the Indian sub-continent receive a large amount of help from agencies worldwide.

The best option for people who want to work in Asia is not to specify a particular country, but a particular region or type of work. Even then, be as flexible as possible.

Types of work available
The main types of work in Asia are disaster relief, medical and health projects, and educational projects.

Sources to use
Apply to UK voluntary agencies or contact Asian agencies direct. A few jobs are advertised in the UK national newspapers and *Overseas Jobs Express*.

Visas and permits
A working visa is required for all these countries and should be applied for from the London Embassy of the relevant country once you have found a job.

Other things you should know
Asia's major cities are generally well developed and, for foreign workers, have similar wages and living costs to the UK. Outside cities, wages and living costs and the general standard of living are much lower. English is widely spoken in most major cities, but not always in other areas.

Useful contacts

UK Voluntary Agencies Working in Asia
Action Water, Mount Hawke, Truro TR4 8BZ. Tel: (01209) 715385.
Aid for India, 186 Cowley Road, Oxford OX4 1UE. Tel: (01865) 728794.
BAM (Freres des Hommes UK), 8 St Michael's Road, London SW9 0SL.
Britain-Nepal Medical Trust, 16 East Street, Tonbridge, Kent TN9 1HG. Tel: (01732) 360284.
British Leprosy Relief Association, Fairfax House, Causton Road, Colchester, Essex CO1 1PU. Tel: (01206) 562286.
CAFOD, Romero Close, Stockwell Road, London SW9 9TY. Tel: (020) 7733 7900.
Christian Outreach, 1 New Street, Leamington Spa CV1 1HP. Tel: (01926) 315301.
Federation of Jewish Relief Organisations, 143 Brondesbury Park, London NW2 5JL. Tel: (020) 8451 3425.
Gordon Barclay Vietnam Fund, 77 Maze Hill, London SE10 8QX. Tel: (020) 8858 4968.

Intermediate Technology Development Group, Myson House, Railway Terrace, Rugby, Warwickshire CV21 3HT. Tel: (01788) 560631.

Impact Foundation, Westview, Lindfield, Sussex RH16 2LJ. Tel: (01444) 483439.

India Development Group, 68 Dowlands Road, Purley, Surrey CR8 4JF. Tel: (020) 8668 3161.

Karuna Trust, 186 Cowley Road, Oxford OX4 1UE. Tel: (01865) 728794.

Medical and Scientific Aid for Vietnam, Laos and Cambodia, 244 Ellerdine Road, Hounslow, Middlesex TW3 2PY. Tel: (020) 8560 1026.

Ockenden Venture, Ockenden, Constitution Hill, Woking, Surrey GU22 7UU. Tel: (01483) 772012.

Oxfam, 274 Banbury Road, Oxford OX2 7DZ. Tel: (01865) 311311.

Pestalozzi Children's Trust, Sedlecombe, Battle, Sussex TN33 0RR. Tel: (01424) 870444.

REDR, 1 Great George Street, London SW1P 3AA. Tel: (020) 7233 3116.

Save the Children Fund, 17 Grove Lane, London SE5 8RD. Tel: (020) 7703 5400.

Tibet Relief Fund UK, 70 Russell Road, London W14 8YL. Tel: (020) 7603 7764.

War on Want, 37-39 Great Guildford Street, London SE1 0ES. Tel: (020) 7620 1111.

WaterAid, 1 Queen Anne's Gate, London SW1H 9BT. Tel: (020) 7233 4800.

World Vision of Britain, Dynchurch House, 8 Abingdon Street, Northampton NN1 2AJ. Tel: (01604) 22964.

Asian Voluntary Agencies Working in Asia

Bangladesh Work Camps Association, 289/2 Work Camps Road, North Shahjahanpur, Dhaka 12, Bangladesh.

Bharat Sevak Samaj, 22 Sardar Patel Road, Chanakyapuri, New Delhi, India.

Indian Volunteers for Community Service, 36 Headstone Road, Harrow, Middx HA1 2PE. Tel: (020) 8863 9544.

Involvement Volunteers Association, PO Box 218, Port Melbourne, Victoria 3207, Australia.

Joint Assistance Centre, H65 South Extension 1, New Delhi 110049, India.

Pakistan Development Corporation, 52-54 High Holborn, London WC1V 6RB.

Paschim Banga Samaj Seva Samity, 191 Chittatanjan Avenue, Calcutta 700007, India.

Sri Lanka Jatika Sarvodaya Shramadana Sangamaya Inc, 98 Rawatawatta Road, Moratuwa, Sri Lanka.

UNESCO Youth Centre, PO Box Central 64, Seoul, Korea.

India

Indian Embassy, India House, Aldwych, London WC2B 4NA. Tel: (020) 7836 8484.

British High Commission, Chanakyapuri, New Delhi 21, 1100-21. Tel: 011 601371.

Indian Tourist Office, 7 Cork Street, London W1X 2AB. Tel: (020) 7629 0862.

Indonesia

Indonesian Embassy, 38 Grosvenor Square, London W1X 9AD. Tel: (020) 7499 7661.

British Embassy, Jalan M.H. Thamrin 75, Jakarta 10310. Tel: 021 330904.

Israel

Israeli Embassy, 2 Palace Green, London W8 4QB. Tel: (020) 7937 8050.

British Embassy, 192 Hayarkon Street, Tel Aviv. Tel: 03 524 9171.

Israel Tourist Office, 18 Great Marlborough Street, London W1V 1AF. Tel: (020) 7434 3651.

Jordan

Jordanian Embassy, 6 Upper Phillimore Gardens, London W8 2HB. Tel: (020) 7937 3685.

British Embassy, Abdoun, PO Box 87, Amman. Tel: 06 823100.

Malaysia

Malaysian High Commission, 45 Belgrave Square, London SW1X 8QT. Tel: (020) 7235 8033.

British High Commission, 185 Jalan Ampang, PO Box 11030, 50732 Kuala Lumpur. Tel: 03 248 2122.

Pakistan

Pakistan High Commission, 35 Lowndes Square, London SW1X 9JN. Tel: (020) 7235 2044.

British High Commission, Ramna 5, PO Box 1122, Islamabad. Tel: 051 822131.

Philippines

Philippines Embassy, 9A Palace Green, London W8 4QE. Tel: (020) 7937 1600.

British Embassy, Locsin Building, 6752 Ayala Avenue, Makati, Metro Manila. Tel: 02 816 7116.

Syria

Syrian Embassy, 8 Belgrave Square, London SW1X 8PH. Tel: (020) 7245 9012.

British Embassy, 11 Rue Mohammed Kurd Ali, Imm. Kotob, Damascus. Tel: 011 712561.

Thailand

Thai Embassy, 30 Queen's Gate, London SW7 5JB. Tel: (020) 7589 0173.

British Embassy, Wireless Road, Bangkok 10330. Tel: 02 235 0191.

Thailand Tourist Office, 9 Stafford Street, London W1X 3FE. Tel: (020) 7499 7679.

AUSTRALIA

About voluntary work in Australia

Although a wealthy country, the situation as regards voluntary work is similar to that in the UK. All the Australian states have reasonably good state provision, but voluntary agencies work in most areas to provide a wide range of important services.

The main difficulty is that it is extremely difficult to obtain a visa for permanent work in and migration to Australia. However, exceptions are made for young people aged 18–25 (sometimes up to 30) who can obtain a 12-month working holiday visa allowing them to take a temporary job in Australia.

Types of work available

All as in Chapter 2. Most voluntary agencies work with the poor and disadvantaged in city areas, particularly the old and disabled, as well as aborigine groups. Environmental and conservation activities are also growing.

Sources to use

It is difficult to arrange jobs in advance and this is best done on arrival. Use newspapers and also direct approaches to employers. It is also a good idea to use private employment agencies and, in Australia, the state employment agency called CES. If a job is arranged in advance (by writing to a charity) this may make it difficult to get a working holiday visa.

Visas and permits

It is extremely difficult to secure permanent residence in Australia. Visas are awarded according to a points system which takes account of your age, status, skills and qualifications. A one-year working holiday visa is much easier to obtain. You must be aged 18–30, with at least £2,000 capital, and intending to stay in Australia for no more than one year and then return. Details are available from the Australian High Commission. It is not possible to get work visas once in Australia.

Other things you should know
Australia has similar costs and standards of living to the UK; wages are about the same or higher.

Useful contacts
Australian High Commission, Australia House, The Strand, London WC2B 4LA. Tel: (020) 7379 4334.
British High Commission, Commonwealth Avenue, Canberra, ACT 2600. Tel: 06 270 6666.
Australian Tourist Commission, Gemini House, 10-18 Putney Hill, London SW15 6AA. Tel: (020) 8780 1424.

Australian Agents-General in London
New South Wales: 75 King William Street, London EC4N 7HA.
Queensland: 392 Strand, London WC2R 0LZ.
South Australia: 50 Strand, London WC2N 5LW.
Victoria: Victoria House, Melbourne Place, Strand, London WC2B 4LG.
Western Australia: 115 Strand, London WC2R 0AJ.

State Employment Services (CES)
45 Grenfell Street, Adelaide.
215 Adelaide Street, Brisbane.
128 Bourke Street, Melbourne.
818-820 George Street, Sydney.
186 St George's Terrace, Perth.

Private Employment Agencies
ECCO, 18 Bent Street, Sydney.
Drake Personnel, 9 Queen Street, Melbourne.

Newspapers
Sydney Morning Herald (Sydney), *Courier & Mail* (Brisbane), *The West Australian* (Adelaide), *The Melbourne Age* (Melbourne).

Voluntary Service Bureaux and Voluntary Agencies
Australian Catholic Relief, 154 Elizabeth Street, Sydney, NSW2000. Tel: 02 264 1592.

Australian Council for the Rehabilitation of the Disabled, PO Box 60, Curtin ACT2605. Tel: 062 824333.

Australian Overseas Disaster Response Organisation, 381 Pitt Street, Sydney NSW2000. Tel: 02 264 9544.

Australian Trust for Conservation Volunteers (ATCV), PO Box 423, Ballarat VIC3350.

Australian Red Cross Society, 206 Clarendon Street, East Melbourne VIC3002. Tel: 03 419 7533.

Christian Work Camps Australia, PO Box 199, Clarance Street, Sydney NSW2000.

International Christian Aid Relief, 45 Stanley Street, Bankstown NSW2200. Tel: 02 708 6107.

Interserve Australia, 7B Ellingworth Parade, PO Box 320, Box Hill VIC3128. Tel: 03 890 0402.

Involvement Volunteers Association, PO Box 218, Port Melbourne, VIC 3207.

National Council of YMCA, 196 Albert Road, South Melbourne, VIC3205. Tel: 03 699 7655.

Overseas Service Bureau, 71 Argyle Street, PO Box 350, Fitzroy, VIC3065. Tel: 03 419 1788.

The Salvation Army, 2 Brisbane Avenue, Barton, Canberra, ACT2600. Tel: 062 733055.

Save the Children Australia, PO Box 281, Collingwood, VIC3066. Tel: 03 417 7662.

Tear Fund Australia, 580 Glenferrie Road, PO Box 289, Hawthorn, VIC 3122. Tel: 03 819 1900.

World Vision of Australia, PO Box 399C, Melbourne VIC3001. Tel: 03 699 8522.

YWCA of Australia, PO Box 309, East Melbourne VIC3002. Tel: 03 417 2131.

Index

OBTAINING VISAS & WORK PERMITS
How and where to obtain the services of immigration lawyers and consultants worldwide

Roger Jones

Today more people than ever are keen to put down roots in foreign countries on either a temporary or long-term basis. But many need advice on how to surmount the many legal obstacles to taking up residence in a foreign land. This unique guide and directory by the author of *How to Emigrate*, lists experts in immigration law and procedures who can guide you through the pitfalls and help you obtain the necessary visas.

140pp. illus. 1 87503 414 7.

WORKING ON CONTRACT WORLDWIDE
How to triple your earnings by working as an independent contractor anywhere in the world

Rod Briggs

Working as a contractor in today's widening international skills market can bring enormous personal financial gain. Earnings can often be treble those of a normal staff salary. Contracting also offers a degree of personal development, professional variety and independence rarely possible in traditionally paid employment. This book is the first to explain in practical steps how to break into the lucrative world of contracting. It explains what 'contracting' means, how to become a contractor yourself, how to cope with the professional, commercial and personal aspects of contracting and how to maximise the opportunities it can offer. Intended originally for engineers, this book will in fact be invaluable for people in almost any profession or discipline. Rod Briggs has himself worked for over 25 years as a contractor in the UK, southern Africa, the Middle East and many countries in western Europe.

160pp. illus. 1 85703 429 5.

PLANNING YOUR GAP YEAR
How to have the time of your life working, studying or travelling

Mark Hempshell

Planning Your Gap Year is a comprehensive guide to planning your year off. It introduces all the exciting possibilities and – best of all – travelling. It explains what you can do, where you can go and is crammed with all the practical information, contacts and addresses you'll need to plan everything and make your gap year an experience you'll remember for the rest of your life. Mark Hempshell is the author of several top selling work-and-travel books and has contributed articles to leading newspapers and magazines. He is the author of *Getting a Job in Europe* now in its fourth edition in this series.

128pp. illus. 1 85703 387 6. 2nd edition.

SPENDING A YEAR ABROAD
How to have the time of your life anywhere around the world

Nick Vandome

A year abroad is now a very popular option among thousands of school leavers, students, and people taking a mid-life break. This book sets out the numerous options available from making the decision to go, to working on a kibbutz, to teaching English as a foreign language, to adapting to life at home on your return. 'Should be required reading…Unlike most reference books this is one which should be read right through, and that is a pleasure as well as being very informative. It is totally comprehensive…very good value for money.' *The School Librarian.* 'Excellent.' *Careers Guidance Today.* Nick Vandome is a young freelance writer who has spent a year abroad on three occasions, in France, Australia, Africa and Asia. His articles have appeared in *The Guardian, The Scotsman, The Daily Telegraph,* and elsewhere.

176pp. illus. 1 85703 544 5. 4th edition.

GETTING A JOB IN AUSTRALIA
A guide to employment opportunities and contacts

Nick Vandome

With ever-increasing competition for entry into Australia and its employment market, it is essential for migrant job-hunters to arm themselves with as much practical and relevant information as possible. This handbook provides a complete step-by-step guide to all aspects of job-finding in Australia, for both casual and permanent employment. 'Very helpful, with details of entry requirements, samples of forms that may be needed, and details on employment law and conditions ranging from national holidays to sexual harassment...Indispensable.' *TNT Magazine.* 'Packed with information which is well presented and easily accessible.' *Bulletin (National Association of Careers & Guidance Teachers).* 'Provides a complete step-by-step guide.' *Australian Outlook.*

190pp. plus. 1 85703 280 2. 3rd edition.

TEACHING ABROAD
How and where to find teaching and lecturing jobs worldwide

Roger Jones

Many professionals today are attracted by the idea of teaching abroad, partly because of all the difficulties that beset teachers in the UK, and partly because of the varied and rewarding opportunities available overseas. Written by a teacher with long experience of foreign postings, this book meets a real demand for practical and realistic information – now thoroughly revised and updated for this third edition. 'Comprehensive and well researched – invaluable' *Education.* 'Recommended.' *Phoenix*/Association of Graduate Careers Advisory Services. Roger Jones is a qualified teacher who taught abroad for more than 12 years. His other books in the series include *Getting a Job in America*, now in its fifth edition.

192pp. illus. 1 85703 276 4. 3rd edition.

GETTING A JOB ABROAD
The handbook for the international jobseeker: where the jobs are, how to get them

Roger Jones

'A highly informative book...containing lots of hard information and a first class reference section.' *The Escape Committee Newsletter*. 'An excellent addition to any careers library... There is a wide range of reference addresses covering employment agencies, specialist newspapers, a comprehensive booklist and helpful addresses...All readers, whether careers officers, young adults or more mature adults will find a use for this book.' *Newscheck*, Careers Services Bulletin.

336 pp. illus. 1 85703 418 X. 5th edition.

MANAGING YOUR PERSONAL FINANCES
How to achieve your own financial security, wealth and independence

John Claxton

Life for most people has become increasingly troubled by financial worries, both at home and at work, whilst the once dependable welfare state is shrinking. This book, now revised and updated, will help you to prepare a strategy towards creating your own financial independence. Find out in simple language: how to avoid debt, how to prepare for possible incapacity or redundancy, and how to finance your retirement, including care in old age. Discover how to acquire new financial skills, increase your income, reduce outgoings, and prepare to survive in a more self-reliant world. John Claxton is a Chartered Management Accountant and Chartered Secretary. He teaches personal money management in adult education.

160pp. illus. 1 85703 471 6. 3rd edition.

GETTING A JOB IN AMERICA
How to find the right employment opportunities and contacts

Roger Jones

A handbook for everyone planning to work in the US, whether on a short-term vacation assignment, secondment or contract, or on a permanent basis. 'Essential for anyone who is thinking of working in the US.' *Going USA.* 'For young people considering a US exchange or summer employment, the section on vacation jobs is particularly worthwhile.' *Newscheck.* 'Very good value for money.' *School Librarian Journal.*

224pp. illus. 1 85703 372 8. 5th edition

BECOMING A CONSULTANT
How to start and run a profitable consulting business

Susan Nash

Consulting has become a lucrative and growing working option. This book will provide you with the methodology to set up and run your own consulting business and an understanding of the steps you need to take to make it successful. It will enable you to define your business's strategic direction and give you the practical skills to make your business a reality. You will learn how to raise finances, maintain financial control, implement a marketing strategy and deliver on-going business. Susan Nash is the British President of EM-Power, a US based consulting firm which has worked with over 50 companies in both the UK and USA. She has presented the workshop 'Consulting and Making Money At It', for the past seven years.

144pp. illus. 1 85703 392 2.